**BRIGHT NOTES**

# DECLINE AND FALL AND OTHER WORKS BY EVELYN WAUGH

**Intelligent Education**

Nashville, Tennessee

BRIGHT NOTES: Decline and Fall and Other Works
www.BrightNotes.com

No part of this publication may be used or reproduced in any manner whatsoever without written permission, except in the case of brief quotations in critical articles and reviews. For permissions, contact Influence Publishers http://www.influencepublishers.com.

ISBN: 978-1-645424-30-7 (Paperback)
ISBN: 978-1-645424-31-4 (eBook)

Published in accordance with the U.S. Copyright Office Orphan Works and Mass Digitization report of the register of copyrights, June 2015.

Originally published by Monarch Press.
Richard K. Brown, 1971
2020 Edition published by Influence Publishers.

Interior design by Lapiz Digital Services. Cover Design by Thinkpen Designs.

Printed in the United States of America.

Library of Congress Cataloging-in-Publication Data forthcoming.
Names: Intelligent Education
Title: BRIGHT NOTES: Decline and Fall and Other Works
Subject: STU004000 STUDY AIDS / Book Notes

# CONTENTS

| | | |
|---|---|---|
| 1) | Introduction to Evelyn Waugh | 1 |
| 2) | Prelude | 9 |
| 3) | Textual Analysis | 11 |
| | Part I | 11 |
| | Part II | 19 |
| | Part III | 24 |
| 4) | Textual Analysis | 28 |
| | Chapter 1 | 28 |
| | Chapter 2 | 30 |
| | Chapter 3 | 33 |
| | Chapter 4 | 36 |
| | Chapter 5 | 38 |
| | Chapter 6 | 41 |
| | Chapter 7 | 44 |
| 5) | Prologue | 46 |
| 6) | Textual Analysis | 48 |
| | Book I | 48 |
| | Book II | 58 |

| | | |
|---|---|---|
| 7) | Textual Analysis | 64 |
| | Chapter 1 | 64 |
| | Chapter 2 | 66 |
| | Chapter 3 | 68 |
| | Chapter 4 | 70 |
| | Chapter 5-6 | 72 |
| | Chapter 7-9 | 74 |
| | Chapter 10 | 75 |
| 8) | Character Analyses | 78 |
| 9) | Essay Questions and Answers | 89 |
| 10) | A Critical Bibliography | 97 |

# INTRODUCTION TO EVELYN WAUGH

## EARLY LIFE, CONVERSION

Upper-class gentility and literary talent were characteristic of the family that welcomed the birth of Evelyn St. John Waugh in London on October 28, 1903. Both parents came from rural families in the social category of "gentry" - landowners, clergymen, doctors, civil servants - who associated with, but were not of, the aristocracy. Evelyn's father, Arthur Waugh, was a professional man of letters - a biographer, poet, and critic - who from 1909 to 1929 was director of the venerable publishing firm of Chapman & Hall. Evelyn's older brother Alec was also literary by nature, and also destined to become a famous writer.

As Evelyn Waugh declares in *A Little Learning*, he had a very happy childhood, assured by the love of his mother and his nurse; he came to appreciate his father only later in life. Before the young Evelyn's formal schooling began, he was steeped in the classics of English poetry and prose, from which his father, an excellent amateur actor, read to him and Alec daily for many years. The effect of these early associations became evident in prep school and at Oxford, where Evelyn was prominent in the literary and debating societies.

After graduation, however, he was obliged to take a job as teacher in a school in Wales (a depressing experience reflected in his **satire** on Dr. Fagan's school in *Decline and Fall*). A publisher's rejection of Waugh's first effort at a novel further depressed him, and he made a half-hearted attempt at suicide, amusingly recorded at the end of *A Little Learning*. This period of melancholy was followed, however, by the success of *Decline and Fall* (1928), a novel that took London by storm. His fame was increased by his next novel, *Vile Bodies* (1930), which satirized the "bright young things" of London society in a way that suggested the moral nihilism of the day.

It was during this period that Waugh became a Roman Catholic, a consequence of the deeply religious temperament that his brother Alec had noted in him at a tender age. After an early marriage ended in divorce, Waugh traveled for ten years throughout the world. His journeys provided him with material for several travel books as well as with background for several novels. *Black Mischief* (1932) brilliantly satirized native African revolution and the European materialism which it parodied; *Scoop* (1936) held the newspaper establishment up to ridicule. Waugh also used his travel experience to provide the South American background for *A Handful of Dust* (1937), which was recognized almost at once as a classic. The year it was published he married again and settled down in the West Country of his ancestors, where he lived most of the rest of his life. This period also saw publication of his *Edmund Campion* (1935), biography of a sixteenth-century Jesuit martyr to religious persecution, which is worthy of study as a model of English prose style, even though its historical perspective may seem biased.

## WARTIME SERVICE, LATER WORKS, DEATH

When World War II broke out, Evelyn Waugh volunteered for the British Royal Marines (in a spirit later attributed to the heroes of both *Brideshead Revisited* and *Men at Arms*). On a troopship en route to the Middle East, Waugh wrote, in the style of his early satires, an "entertainment" called *Put Out More Flags* (1943) in which Basil Seal, rascal-hero of *Black Mischief*, reappears as a conniving war-profiteer. A lesser work, *Put Out More Flags* nevertheless ends on a note of patriotic affirmation as Basil volunteers for the armed forces.

After seeing action with the Commandos in the Middle East, and serving on a special mission to Yugoslavia, Waugh returned home to compose (in what he later referred to as a nostalgic mood) *Brideshead Revisited*. A departure from his earlier work in its lavish evocative style and romantic attitudes, it is also the first work in which his religious beliefs appear as the affirmation of a moral norm. The novel is purportedly a fictional representation of the process of conversion. It is generally and justly regarded by Waugh's critics as an inferior work, but it enjoyed an enormous popular success and brought him worldwide fame.

As a result, after the war Waugh made a trip to Hollywood at the expense of a major studio; once there, he refused them permission to film *Brideshead Revisited*. Instead, he collected material for his next book by visiting a famous cemetery and by observing life in Los Angeles. The result of this excursion was *The Loved One* (1948), a brilliant **satire** of the more outlandish aspects of American mortuary practices. Superior to *Brideshead Revisited* as a literary work, it repeated the latter's popular success, bringing Waugh an acclaim such as he would never again attain.

In the remaining twenty-odd years of his life, spent mainly among his growing family, he continued to produce works notable for their originality, variety, and quality, including:

*Helena* (1950), a fictional and openly "apologetic" version of the life of St. Helen, mother of Constantine and founder of the True Cross; *The Ordeal of Gilbert Pinfold* (1957), a fascinating and at times hilarious fictional account of Waugh's own nervous breakdown; and his final major work, the trilogy of World War II - *Men at Arms* (1952), *Officers and Gentlemen* (1955), and *Unconditional Surrender* (1961), published together as *Sword of Honour* (1965) - in which the hero, Guy Crouchback, embodies traditional values. In addition, Waugh wrote the authorized biography of *Monsignor Ronald Knox*, translator of the Bible and a lifelong friend, whose prose style Waugh modestly considered superior to his own. Finally, Waugh completed *A Little Learning* (1964), the first volume of his projected autobiography. He died suddenly after a brief illness in April 1966, already recognized as one of the greatest stylists in English literature.

## NOVELIST AND SATIRIST

### Periods of Development

Evelyn Waugh's career as one of the major satirists of the twentieth century falls into two main periods, with World War II as the line of demarcation. The first period corresponds to the years between the two great wars, the Great Armistice of 1919-1939. It includes (considering only the fiction) *Decline and Fall, Vile Bodies, Black Mischief,* and *Scoop,* all of which might be characterized as satiric fantasies; and *A Handful of Dust*, possibly the finest example of sustained **irony** in the English language. This period can be justly described as one of steady development of control over his material and perfection of style. The second, postwar period of 1945-1965, begins with *Brideshead Revisited*, a departure from previous works in both style and purpose, and rightly described as a realistic romance.

The second period, however, also includes the most brilliant of Waugh's satiric fantasies, *The Loved One*, as well as some minor examples of the same genre; among these, Scott King's *Modern Europe* and Love *Among The Ruins*, both socio-political in nature. Completed also in this period were a highly original historical novel of the legendary St. Helen; and the major trilogy on World War II, *Sword of Honour*. This last is a generally underrated work which, with at least partial success, combines his earlier satiric manner with realistic treatment of social and religious problems. Waugh's second period, therefore, may be characterized as one of continuous expansion of range in the variety of literary forms and styles, a development that is nevertheless still based essentially on his satiric purpose and method.

## Satire and The Satiric Norm

To understand Waugh's artistic development, we must have some appreciation of the basic concept of **satire**. That satire makes fun of something or someone is widely recognized, but what this implies is not so readily understood. First of all, the colloquial "makes fun of" carries the sense of mockery or ridicule; but to ridicule someone, to make him appear ridiculous, is to indicate some kind of disapproval, which in turn suggests that a judgment has been made. But a judgment requires some kind of standard or norm, against which a person's action is measured, and a deviation from this norm is the cause of disapproval and condemnation. Thus, the satirist is essentially a moralist; that is, he is concerned with people's mores, or people's behavior and the codes that regulate it. However, the satirist's norm is not necessarily a moral code in the sense of the Golden Rule or the Ten Commandments, though it might well be based on one. His norm is rather the social expression of some such moral system as it affects people's relationships with one another; for example, the relationship of two people involved in a divorce suit, the conduct of which is determined by the divorce laws. These laws, and the whole situation, have reference to a concept of marriage, but this concept is not necessarily the norm of the satirist; he might ridicule those involved in the divorce because, for example, by the standard of the divorce laws, the contestants are dishonest. Such is the case in *A Handful of Dust*. Or the norm might be one associated with a particular social group or class, as, for example, the ideal of the "gentleman" associated with the "gentry" or upper-class - an ideal of courtly behavior that historically originates in the specifically religious vows of chivalry. This ideal of the gentleman is present in most of Waugh's writings. It can be seen, then, that **satire** (as distinct from mere farce, which of course can serve a satiric intention) has two essential characteristics: (1) It is social - that is, it has to do with the relationships of people in their social existence, and (2) it is moral - that is, it makes fun of people's actions with reference to a norm and thereby judges and, usually, either implicitly or explicitly, condemns them.

To understand completely the satirist's intention it is therefore necessary to recognize the norm or standard of judgment by which he represents something as "ridiculous." And quite often this norm will be embodied by the satirist in some representative who affirms the positive values that the "ridiculous" characters deny. Sometimes, however, the norm is implicit (not directly stated) and difficult to identify unless we have some idea of the specifically literary traditions and forms, as distinct from moral codes, that the satirist employs for his purpose. Here is where the study of literary history enables us to understand the significance of what otherwise might appear insignificant or even irrelevant. An example from classical literature may perhaps help to clarify this point. One of the most ancient literary traditions, originating in early Greek poetry and persisting, through poetry, drama, and prose fiction, in various forms to the present day is the pastoral. The term itself (Latin pastor: shepherd) suggests an association with nature. Early Greek lyric poets like Bion and Theocritus, who celebrated the idyllic existence - the ideal of man's harmony with nature - used the shepherd as representative of this ideal. Thus the pastoral idyll celebrated life in harmony with one's natural surroundings, which presumably were conducive to virtue (or at least the "virtues" of simplicity, frugality, and the like). Later poets like Virgil, however, held up this ideal as a contrast to the corruption of society as distinct from nature (a corruption associated with life in the city) and, through contrast, implicitly satirized such corruption. This satiric use of the pastoral tradition was imitated by writers of the Renaissance and was thereby incorporated into English literature, where it continued into modern prose fiction, beginning with Henry Fielding's *Joseph Andrews*. And so in American literature, Mark Twain in *Huckleberry Finn* employs the pastoral tradition when he contrasts the idyllic freedom of Huck and Jim's life on the raft with the corrupt slaveholding society on the shore. So also in *The Great Gatsby*, F. Scott Fitzgerald associated the American West, the Frontier, with pastoral virtue and the East with social corruption.

Having seen how a specific literary tradition can be variously employed for satiric purposes, we come to the question of how we can apply our general observations to the works of Evelyn Waugh. From the foregoing, it is clear that we must attempt first to identify the norm - or at least determine if there is one. As has been indicated, the norm may be either explicitly embodied in some figure (or even some institution or ideal) in the narrative; or it may be implicitly contained in, for example, some contrast of opposites - loyalty by disloyalty, traditional values by their denial, and so forth. In Waugh's case, the problem is complicated by the fact that his output comprises such a variety of literary **genres** or forms - sometimes in one work - that it is difficult to distinguish the significant from the incidental. The problem is further complicated by the fact that in some instances the norm is present only intermittently, if at all; in others it is implicit, and in at least one case there is an explicit norm but practically no **satire**! There is, however, in his work an overall development from lack of any clearly discernible norm in the earliest **satires** to either an implicit or explicit norm in his later works. This can be illustrated by examining the four major works analyzed in this text as examples of phases of this development.

After our detailed study of these four novels, we shall be in a better position to discuss Waugh's growth as an artist.

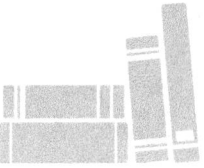

# DECLINE AND FALL

## PRELUDE

..............................................................

### JUXTAPOSITION - CIVILIZATION AND BARBARISM

The opening of the novel - a forecast of some of the most hilarious satiric writing in twentieth-century literature - is an excellent illustration of Waugh's basic comic method as well as the problems it raises. The method itself is simply a version of the age-old structural principle of juxtaposition, or the contrast of two unlike things by placing them side by side, thus effecting the incongruity which is the essence of all comedy. That is, the recognition of the incongruous is the recognition of the difference between what something or someone is supposed to be (or pretends to be), and what it or he actually is; and this recognition of the truth, as the classic statement puts it, "surprises us into laughter." In this instance, of course, the incongruity is between what we expect the traditionally staid and even stuffy Oxford dons and students (not to mention aristocrats) to be, and what they are at least pictured to be. The element of exaggeration, which is common to farce, is deliberately used to heighten the effect, and is admissible so long as it does not detract from this effect. The resulting farcical picture of life at Oxford is acceptable to us if it has a possible basis in what might be considered some form of "barbarism" existing - and even encouraged or protected - in what is presumably the very center of civilization, the university. The problem arises when we attempt to locate in the action some unambiguous representation of "civilization" against which the "barbarism" may be measured and judged. For instance, representatives of the university are callous and actively unjust; the representative of the Church is indifferent to the hero's fate; and his serious fellow-theologians are a pitiably small and ineffectual minority. At the same time, the positive values of order, discipline, and learning that could be represented by art are associated with a few students who, it is suggested, are mere eccentrics. In short, the standard by which the satirist both judges and ridicules the barbaric, as a deviation from the norm, is itself contradictory and consequently ambiguous. And this basic ambiguity is, in fact, true of the rest of the novel.

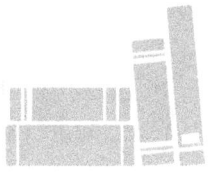

# DECLINE AND FALL

## TEXTUAL ANALYSIS

## PART I

### CHAPTERS 1-4

#### Naifs and Grotesques

More than one critic has observed that Waugh's works exhibit a wide variety of characters - or, more precisely, types of characters. James F. Carens attempts to classify these types in his fine study, *The Satiric Art of Evelyn Waugh* (see Bibliography). He places Waugh's characters in three general categories: (1) ingenus, or naifs, (2) subsidiary figures associated with them, and finally (3) the grotesques. The "heroes," like Paul Pennyfeather, usually belong to the first category; they are naive, or innocent of the corruption of the world, and much of the **satire** is effected by the contrast between their innocence and that corruption. (Classic examples of this ingenu type are Voltaire's *Candide* and Twain's *Huckleberry Finn*.) The naifs' associates, though important figures in the story, are not innocent; both heroes and associates, however, invariably belong to the upper classes.

Unlike the grotesques, both are also characterized by means of understatement - by a few suggestive details that are then completed in dialogue and action.

This classification of the hero as a naif is more applicable to the earlier **satires** like *Decline and Fall* than to a transitional work like a *Handful of Dust* or the later *Brideshead Revisited*; though in a certain sense the heroes of these later works are innocent, and the narratives reveal the process of their discovery of reality. The grotesques, on the other hand, are almost all from the lower, or nonaristocratic classes, and their portrayal is by the classic method of caricature (the exaggeration of a single trait to the exclusion of all others) so that they become representations of the dominant trait rather than of credible human beings. In short, they are "fantastic." Grimes and Prendergast, two other teachers at Llanaba, both belong to this general category of grotesque, and it is again in the contrast of this category with the nongrotesque or "real" that Waugh attains his satiric effects. However, we should not assume that the categories are absolutely fixed. Later on, in their dealings with the school butler, Philbrick, Grimes and Prendergast tend to shift into the same category as Paul, since Philbrick turns out to be even more "fantastic" than the others.

## CHAPTERS 5-7

### Narrative Structure

These three chapters constitute a microcosm of the basic narrative pattern of the novel. Though the action appears rather disconnected - an impression that the author deliberately fosters to encourage the sense of chaos he wishes to convey - it can be seen that each division is organized around some kind of event which fits into a larger chronological sequence. Likewise, there are in each division references to past and future, even if not always immediate, that help to establish a sense of time that recalls the past or anticipates the future. Chapter Six is obviously less "chronological" than he others - that is, it isn't necessarily restricted to a particular point in the time-sequence, but could be placed somewhere else without violating the sequence.

## CHAPTERS 8-10

### Aristocrats and Snobs

The arbitrary division of the Sports Day event into three chapters is obviously a deliberate device on the part of the author. What is not so obvious at first is the reason for the device, and a consideration of the possible reason will tell us something about the author's intention. The basic intention here, as throughout the whole book, is clearly satiric - the people involved in the event are being ridiculed. But there must be some kind of recognizable frame of reference or standard for **satire** to be completely effective. As we know, it is possible for some individual satiric point - some specific spoken line or action - to be effective, that is, to show up some proper object of ridicule such as pretense or deceit. But this effect depends precisely on some assumed standard common to author and reader, or, at the very least, a coincidental unspoken agreement (even if based on different standards) that something is ridiculous. For we must remember that even the most primitive form of slapstick comedy depends on a common recognition of, for instance, the human limitations that are illustrated when someone falls on his face. This point is worth dwelling on here, since it helps us to understand that the arbitrary division of the main event of Part I serves to emphasize the "climax," and thereby assumes a standard of judgment on the part of the reader that can only be described as snobbery or bigotry. That is, this arrangement of the chapters would not be necessary to emphasize the shock or dismay (arising from snobbery or bigotry) on the part of the characters in the story - and their reactions are in fact revealed in the following chapter. Rather, the arrangement is clearly intended to shock the reader, who would just as clearly not be shocked if he did not share the prejudice of the characters - and, it may be added, of the author himself.

Now, much has been made of Waugh's undeniable "aristocratic" bias: his stated belief in the superiority of the English upper-class and the traditional hierarchy of a titled aristocracy and monarchy. (It was this same bias that made his adopted religion of Roman Catholicism especially congenial to him.) It might therefore logically follow that Waugh judges and derides those taking part in Sports Day for deviating from some norm of ideal aristocratic conduct - some gentlemanly code of honor.

The trouble is, however, that no such code is evident in anything either Paul or anyone else says or does in the whole course of the day; nor is it implicit in any reference to ethical or religious values. It is simply nonexistent. For example, although the mockery of the black man's plea for equality mocks the "phony" black man and is balanced by the picture of white race hatred, there is a lack of any normative concept of compassion or integrity; and the evidence of other (though less extensive) racial or national slurs in this part of the novel contributes further to a feeling of racial snobbery. At times, the narrative suggests a tone of contemptuous scorn, as if Waugh is sneering at the whole of humanity. Nor does a certain callousness to the suffering of children add much, even in farcical treatment, other than an uneasiness about the satirist's attitude. In short, despite the brilliance of individual parts, the overall impression we receive of the Annual Sports Day is not so much of the folly of mankind being ridiculed in the hope of ultimate correction, as of the author's failure to reveal or imply any coherent code of proper behavior or the cultural values that could sustain such behavior.

## Point of View

An aspect of technique evident as we progress through the novel is point of view. It should be made clear at once that this is not the attitude of the author toward his material that we have referred to above, but is, rather, the specific angle of narration from which the story is told. There are many variations open to the writer, but these can all be reduced to three basic kinds. The first is the so-called all-knowing or omniscient author; here the writer narrates the story in his own voice, grammatically in the third person, intruding whenever he wishes to address the reader directly to comment on the events of his own narrative. The obvious advantage of this method is that the narrator can move freely back and forth in time and space, from one scene to another, even if events are simultaneous, and can pause to interpret the motives of his characters. This angle of narration also establishes a sense of distance in the reader, who looks down with the author in godlike fashion on the panorama of the action, and it is therefore the most objective narrative angle. This point of view is most suitable for the satirist, who wishes to present an exterior picture of his characters (through their actions) rather than an interior one (through their thoughts).

The second kind of point of view is the most subjective, in that it is told entirely from the angle of the "I" narrator, and so is called the first person point of view. The advantage of this subjectivity is the sense it imparts to the reader of immediate participation in the narrated events; the obvious disadvantage is that, when strictly observed, it is of necessity restricted to what the "I" narrator can recall having seen or heard about. The third kind of point of view to some extent, though not entirely, overcomes this limitation and combines the advantages of first person and omniscient author. It is in the third person grammatically, narrates objectively what "he" or "she" does and thinks, but it is also restricted to what is seen or thought by one (or more) characters participating in the action and so is called the single or restricted consciousness.

In *Decline and Fall*, the overall point of view is that of the author omniscient. That is, though much of the action is seen as if exclusively through Paul's consciousness, this is not always the case. We see Waugh, when it suits his purpose, shifting from single consciousness to omniscient and back, thereby combining the advantages of each, namely, immediacy and objectivity. In Chapter 10, we can see the author employing point of view to forward his satiric plot without concerning himself with the motives of the character. In a purely omniscient manner, he allows us to overhear conversations, but refuses to share his characters' thoughts with us. Waugh, even while creating an illusion that we are sharing Paul's experience, and thereby giving the reader a sense of verisimilitude (or likeness to reality), is in fact avoiding the question of the characters' motivation and is concentrating solely on the development of his plot, which alone has any significance. Thus, at this stage in his career Waugh is writing solely as a satirist, concerned only with the significance of people's actions, which he represents in a basically farcical plot. It is only later in his development - beginning, as we shall see, with *A Handful of Dust* - that he begins to move away from "pure" **satire**, and its preoccupation with exterior action, toward realistic romance, in which he is concerned with the psychology of human behavior - that is, motivation.

## CHAPTERS 11-13

### Grotesques and Gentlemen

The last chapters of Part One serve the function of tying up all the loose ends. But they are also and essentially concerned with Philbrick and Grimes as kinds of characters, and they serve, too, to bring out points related to Waugh's general satiric intention.

What precisely does Philbrick's "history" have to do with the satire, especially as it has such a tenuous connection with the plot? The answer might be found in an examination of Philbrick's tales - by trying to ascertain, first, whether they have anything in common. In two versions of the tales, we notice, two common points occur: the reason for Philbrick's wealth and status and the reason for his presence (incompatible with his position) at the castle. In one version, Philbrick is at the castle as an act of penance; in another version he is there in expiation of sins against his family ties. Such are the common elements that Philbrick's tales can be reduced to, but what indeed are they about? Again, the pattern is evident upon comparison: they are all about a man of exceptional ability (and of earned or inherited wealth) who deigns to dwell among his inferiors to satisfy his own special sense of honor. It is obviously a myth of self-approval created by a disordered mind; but it is also a **parody** - an imitation in grotesque form - of a romance whose hero is a gentleman-in-disguise (not too far from the *Count of Monte Cristo* and *Robin Hood*, among others). What is suggested, then, is some kind of **satire** of an ideal code of conduct that is consciously held by a man of refinement superior to the "lower classes," not of (though associated with) the aristocracy. It is also possible to suggest that the gentleman's code (and class) has been so corrupted by impersonators that a fantastic figure like Philbrick can exist and perpetrate his deceptions on the innocent or the ignorant. This suggestion is tenable and agrees with the author's celebrated class prejudice, but again in the context of the whole work, there is no explicit formulation or implicit embodiment of such a class ideal that provides a standard that would enable the reader, by contrast, to recognize Philbrick's significance.

Grimes, though he qualifies as grotesque, is more complex as a character, though less successful than Philbrick as a satirical figure. Waugh has declared that if in creating literary characters he transcribed actual people literally, they would not be believable, since real human beings are too complex and contradictory; thus he defends what we have called his "grotesques" as a more effective representation of reality. There are two points that should be noted about this observation. One is that when Waugh says this, he is thinking essentially about satiric representation, which shows us the difference between the appearance and the reality. The other point is that to be successfully portrayed, such a fantastic character must be entirely consistent and, since his traits are exaggerated, relatively simple; but Grimes, in the last few chapters of Part One, is neither. His pretension to being a "public-school [prep school] man," and therefore a gentleman, is ridiculed by his obvious deviation from the accepted norm and by his complacent self-satisfaction at being incorrigibly amoral. However, he soon grows conscious of his limitations and sensitive to criticism, and so he becomes a figure more pathetic than comic. Yet part of Grimes' long speech is an extended joke, a **parody** of the kind of serious reflection that would require a fanciful mind, conscious of the real values that Grimes is supposedly unaware of. The fact is that this speech is a jeu d'esprit - a witticism on the author's part - for which Grimes is merely the mouthpiece. All of this, then, adds up to an inconsistency in the representation of Grimes as a grotesque, indicating the author's lack of complete control of his material as a satiric artist.

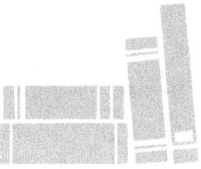

# DECLINE AND FALL

## TEXTUAL ANALYSIS

## PART II

### CHAPTER 1

#### Past and Present

Waugh has a lot of fun, at this point in the narrative, with what is to become one of his major, lifelong **themes** - the superiority of the past over the present. Behind the fun he is deadly serious, since what he is expressing in his satiric contrast is essentially his fear of the destruction, by the mindless nihilism of the present, of the cultural values inherited from the past. To express this fear, he employs one of his major interests, domestic architecture, and here, for the first time, introduces the motif of the *Great House* (King's Thursday) that is perhaps the major symbol in his writing - especially notable, as we shall see, in *A Handful of Dust* and again in *Brideshead Revisited*. If we substitute for King's Thursday something like Pre-Victorian England, (or, more generally, the period before the Industrial Revolution) and for Professor Silenus' ideal, the twentieth century, the import of the contrast becomes clearer. Waugh regards this past era, with all its admitted physical hardships, as spiritually more congenial to mankind, especially in its recognition of the need for beauty in human life (as manifested in the most magnificent form of dwelling). Waugh sees the present, despite its physical conveniences, as spiritually ugly and desolated by the inhuman worship of the machine - a worship resulting in a mass civilization in which people are only a means to power. Now, there is nothing profound and certainly nothing new to us in these ideas, but we should remember that this warning, embodied in a "light" **satire**, was written just a few years before Adolf Hitler came to power (just as, a few years later, his second satiric novel, *Vile Bodies*, ended on the battlefield of a universal war, less than ten years before World War II). Also, we should especially note that here, in an individual section, the **satire** is perfect; for King's Thursday provides the standard by which the target of **satire**, the wanton destruction of beauty, appears obviously ridiculous. But again, Waugh's success is limited to this one effect and, as it exemplifies the author's control, it reveals by contrast the lack of such control throughout the rest of the book.

## CHAPTER 2

### The Vanishing Hero

In his excellent study of the novelists of the twenties, called *The Vanishing Hero*, the Irish author Sean O'Faolain observes of Evelyn Waugh's early novels (by which he means those before *Brideshead Revisited*) that Waugh wanted to imply the norm by which his characters were ridiculed, and so deliberately refrained from embodying the norm in any central figure or hero. The observation may be just, but if we examine carefully how Waugh portrays his own non-hero in Chapter 2, we may find some contradiction of O'Faolain's thesis in Waugh's stated intention. Here, Paul Pennyfeather is put into his proper place in reality and considered for a moment in that perspective. Seen thus, he is clearly inappropriate for the role that is usually indicated by the term "hero." Paul holds no interest for us in himself; he is the "hero" only in the sense that he is the central figure in a narrative in which what happens is alone significant. Now, what Waugh seems to be saying here is that, aside from gentlemanly conduct, Paul in his solid bourgeois reality is incapable of embodying a norm. That is to say, his principles of conduct (which are restricted to his own social class) are too superficial and limited to be universally valid as a standard for judging the conduct of others. Thus, Waugh seems to indicate that such a standard, if there is one, is to be found elsewhere in the narrative itself.

## CHAPTER 3

### Style and Diction

The major characteristic of Waugh's style can be called its economy. As we would say, "Not a word is wasted." But our primary concern is how Waugh manages his material to attain this economy. Sean O'Faolain, in his essay on Waugh in *The Vanishing Hero*, attributes the success of Waugh's style to his use of what O'Faolain calls the "eclectic adjective" - a descriptive word that includes diverse elements, thus concentrating the satiric meaning. If, for instance, one describes a character as stiff-backed and pompous as an alderman, much is conveyed to us indirectly about the character, and we are left to assume the rest. But such usage is not the only factor in stylistic economy. Style is, of course, primarily a matter of language; and the diction, or quality of the words used, is a basic element. So also, however, is the composition of words into the larger units, sentences. The critic, Christopher Hollis, among others, has observed in his study of Waugh (*Writers and Their Work Series*, No. 46) that Waugh's "early style," referring to the period before *Brideshead Revisited*, is notable for its short, simple sentences. While we do find some long rhythmic sentences in *Decline and Fall*, it is still true that this early style is basically simpler than the style that develops later, especially in *Brideshead Revisited*. The simplicity by no means disappears as though Waugh changed abruptly, but in the latter work, we find a greater use of figures of speech - **similes** and **metaphors** - and a more extensive and complex use of **imagery**. So it is not merely the kinds of words and the way he uses them that contribute to Waugh's seemingly simple style in *Decline and Fall*; it is also a matter of what he leaves out or implies. The style is essentially that of indirection. It is, therefore, in the combination of **diction** and suggestion in description, dialogue, and narration that Waugh attains the economy of style that contributes so greatly to the effectiveness of his satire.

## CHAPTERS 4-6

### Naifs, Grotesques, and Verisimilitude

As was suggested earlier, the "real" Paul Pennyfeather is incapable of being heroic in the sense of embodying some standard by which the conduct of the other characters in the novel could be judged and thereby ridiculed. But there is another, and even stronger, reason that the "real" Paul Pennyfeather has no place in the narrative in which, the author says, he is a mere "shadow." The reason is precisely this shadow's special function in the **satire**. For satire to be most effective, generally speaking, the characters must be simple. This is not to say that they must be incredible, rather than they must be credible on the level of the narrative. This means that they must be consistent enough not to contradict the illusion of reality or verisimilitude that the writer of fiction aims to create. The more a character is like a real person, the more complex and self-contradictory he naturally becomes; and the more likely he is to be less "coherent" than a simple character who, so to speak, fits into the illusion. So in this particular likeness to reality, which is on the level of farce, it is perfectly appropriate for Paul to be a naif whose innocence provides the basis for the action. Thus, for example, it is extremely unlikely that the "real" Paul Pennyfeather, described earlier, would be so naive as not to recognize that Margot is engaged in international prostitution or "white slavery." On the other hand, since the character of Paul is kept consistently simple, with the emphasis on his naivete, the reader is willing to accept his blindness, especially in view of his infatuation with Margot, to all of the hints that the reader has easily put together. Furthermore, since we accept the farcical level of the action, we are not too surprised at the reappearance of Grimes and Prendergast, two grotesque characters who prefigure the preposterous events which will follow. Finally, in keeping with the farce (which is "like reality" only as an imitation of its most ridiculous aspects), Margot is never allowed to become any more complex than the others, though she is neither a naif nor a grotesque. Indeed, her motivation is left so unexplored that there is a question in the reader's mind whether she has framed Paul or not, but this is left unresolved since it is unrelated to the satiric purpose. In brief, then, we can see that Waugh's characterization is suited to his satiric purpose, and that the nature of the characters is determined entirely by the function in the narrative.

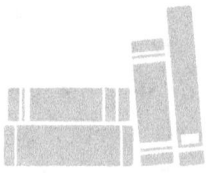

# DECLINE AND FALL

## TEXTUAL ANALYSIS

### PART III

................................................................

#### CHAPTERS 1-5

**Snobbery and Satire**

These five chapters form a unit, for they present a continuous, connected narrative; at the same time, they bring to an end the hero's relationships with three major characters in preparation for the conclusion of the narrative as a whole. They also perfectly exemplify the purely farcical level of satire. But behind their brilliant hilarity, there are some assumptions that are of considerable interest to the student of **satire** and of Waugh's writings in particular. The chapters involving the comic prison-warden satirize modern attempts at reform of the Penal Code. If crime, as the warden thinks, is merely the result of the insane carpenter's artistic frustrations, then the entire contemporary trend toward prison reform is ludicrous. And it is in such ways that Waugh ridicules the modern world. That the mad carpenter's act of murder is the result of an insane attempt to apply irrelevant principles to a practical human problem is self-evident to all of us, and our response is based on the common norm of simple logic. Nor is Prendergast's death to be regarded as gruesome or as evidence of the author's sadism, since it is the perfectly appropriate conclusion of the joke, and quite suitable to Prendergast's function as a farcical character.

But a careful examination of the farcical events strongly suggests that the reader's universal norm of common sense is not necessarily identical with Waugh's norm. For example, Waugh indicates more than once that Lucas-Dockery should leave well enough alone, that the Penal Code as it stands contains the accumulated wisdom of traditional society and should not be meddled with by dangerous fools. In short there is an assumption that things as they are is the best way for them to be, in view of permanent human failings; an assumption that also accepts as inevitable and even right the division of society into strictly differentiated classes, and that holds the class of ladies and gentlemen to be naturally superior. In other words, the writer's implied norm, in this case, is snobbery. The same assumption is articulated in the section on Margot, where that lady, despite her corruption, is seen as the epitome of the upper classes. Paul considers her as literally beyond the law - a doctrine resembling the idea of Superman by which Raskolnikov justifies murder in *Crime and Punishment.* Of course, the doctrine is here presented lightly, but it is nevertheless explicit. Nor can it be argued that it is Paul's snobbery, alone, that is being satirized because there is no apparent standard with which to contrast - and implicitly condemn - his assumption of Margot's unquestionable superiority. Therefore, even though, again, the norm is restricted to a particular section of the whole narrative, it seems quite evident that Waugh's norm is the very limited one of snobbery; and the success of the **satire** is the result of an accidental agreement of his norm with the reader's universal norm of common sense.

## CHAPTER 6, 7 AND EPILOGUE

### The Final Word

The epilogue structurally balances the prelude at the opening of the narrative, bringing the whole full circle to the point where it began. Both in the last full chapter and in the epilogue there is an explicit reference to a norm or standard of order by which to measure Paul's experience of disorder - a disorder presented in as much fantastic detail as possible in the interest of a certain gross and comic verisimilitude.

In his essay on Waugh in *The Vanishing Hero*, Sean O'Faolain maintained that Waugh deliberately refrained from embodying the norm in the central figure, or "hero," preferring instead to imply a universal standard that all readers would assume for themselves. But as we have indicated, at several points in the narrative there is evidence to contradict this thesis. Waugh, himself, strongly suggests that Paul, in his "real" character as a gentleman, is incapable of embodying a universal norm, since his code of conduct is too restricted to have such universal application. But neither can we find with any consistency throughout the novel an implied universal norm. In certain sections of the narrative, Waugh's implied norm is snobbery. This is hardly universal, however, and the **satire** in these sections is, in fact, effective only because this norm happens, by nature of the farcical action, to coincide with the universal standard of common sense.

It is only in the last chapter and epilogue that there is any attempt to establish a standard that might be universally valid. The attempt takes two forms. One clear implication is that people should be content to live within the limits of their own natures. But this, though universal in its application, is a purely pragmatic concept that merely provides a modus vivendi, or satisfactory way of life. The second attempt at indicating a universal standard (never adequately established throughout the narrative) is by contrasting Paul's ordered and specifically religious existence with the disorder of essentially irreligious existence. But even more explicit are the two **allusions** to the condemnation of unorthodoxy by religious authority. In one, heresies are condemned for their denial of truth; in the other, for a practice based on illusion rather than reality (a form of idolatry). Both examples, it should be observed, clearly approve of an ultimate authority embodied in a traditional institution by which all must govern their conduct, or civilization itself, it is implied, will perish. So we can conclude that Waugh finally does attempt to establish a norm of order on which to base his **satire** of disorder, but we see, also, that it is inadequately embodied in the narrative as a whole. *Decline and Fall*, then, though obviously indicative of its author's comic genius, is artistically immature **satire** because the author is not yet in complete control of his material - the ridiculous aspects of human behavior.

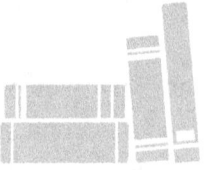

# A HANDFUL OF DUST

## TEXTUAL ANALYSIS

### CHAPTER 1

#### STRUCTURE AND CONTRAST

As a glance at the table of contents would indicate, though the chapters are of unequal length and unequally subdivided, these major divisions of the structure of *A Handful of Dust* have a certain symmetry. From the chapter titles alone, it is evident that the author is deliberately employing one of the most venerable principles of construction in the form of the novel, that of antithesis, or contrast. Such contrast immediately suggests comparisons between one part of the work and another and warns the reader to be aware of other kinds of contrasts throughout the work. We see that Waugh immediately and subtly establishes the contrast between the Beavers' pretense to gentility and their parasitic existence. This contrast is emphasized by the use of a French phrase that is associated with a grand establishment. When the same phrase is later used for a location in the jungle, there is an unavoidable implication of the "civilized" savagery of people like Beaver. This kind of meaningful contrast of parts is lacking in the earlier *Decline and Fall*, where although there are repeated chapter headings, they are merely whimsical references to the action and not symmetrically balanced. This increased awareness of structure is evidence of Waugh's greater control of his material. From the first, we see the author deliberately employing contrast for implied comparisons which will enable us to interpret his intention.

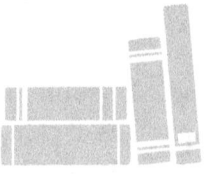

# A HANDFUL OF DUST

## TEXTUAL ANALYSIS

### CHAPTER 2

#### THE GREAT HOUSE

One of the recurrent images in Waugh's work is that of the great country home, or manor-house, of the titled aristocracy or of the "gentry" - the wealthy upper class associated with the nobility. (As titled landowners, the two are often identical, but not necessarily.) In his earliest work, *Decline and Fall*, Waugh uses the Tudor manor-house, King's Thursday, as a symbol of the values of the past that are being destroyed by modern society. And in the present instance, Hetton Abbey also represents these values - reverence for the past, dignity, tradition, and stability - at least to Tony. But these values are also tied to a medieval feudal system of society; they represent an ideal of the past that is impossible to maintain in the modern world with its different economic and social conditions. So that, in living as he does in this ideal world, Tony is living in a dream-world instead of reality. This is revealed quite subtly, for example, in Tony's mode of attendance at church. Church going is part of his own private ritual, performed because it is traditional in his family, not because it is meaningful in itself; during the services Tony thinks mainly of repairs to the house. The sermon, itself, is comically irrelevant to the lives of the parishioners, who tolerate the whole performance because it is traditional.

Tony is recognizable as a type of character called a naif, or innocent. In the literature of **satire**, and in Waugh's early satires like *Decline and Fall*, and *Scoop*, the naivete, or innocence, of the hero is contrasted with the corruption of the world around him, producing comic results which satirize the corruption. Here, however, the hero's naivete is of a subtler kind, tied as it is to the peculiar ideal represented by the Great House; and, again, unlike the earlier satires, where the hero's development is incidental, here the process of the hero's disillusionment with the ideal is central to the narrative.

## FANTASY, TRUTH AND SATIRE

In his essay, "Mr. Waugh's Cities," included in a collection of critical essays on modern literature, *Puzzles and Epiphanies*, Frank Kermode states his considered opinion that *A Handful of Dust* is one of the most distinguished novels of the twentieth century. In commenting on this novel, Kermode observes that the Christmas sermon exemplifies Waugh's balance of "truth and fantasy," and goes on to develop the idea that truth is the "silent context" of fantasy. That is to say, the truth (which in this case includes the positive values of Waugh's religious belief) is never stated explicitly, but is clearly implied by the fantasy. But the term fantasy as Mr. Kermode employs it (without completely defining it) is not precise. By its opposition to truth, he suggests that the story, the plot or action of the novel, is untrue - or more exactly, perhaps, unreal. In addition he says of the same work that viciousness and corruption are depicted as "farcically funny." Kermode's total suggestion, then, of unreality and farce, gives the impression that *A Handful of Dust* - even if more perfected as a work of art - is essentially on the same level, as, for example, *Decline and Fall*. But the level of the action of *Decline and Fall* is sheer farce, marked by the quality of exaggeration that identifies the farcical, and it is not intended to be literally credible. This is not true of *A Handful of Dust*, although like *Decline and Fall* it is a **satire**. The characters are represented as "real" - not incredible; unlike farcical caricatures, they act out of recognizable human motives, and they exist in a "real" world. The Vicar, for instance, though he is obviously eccentric, is not so much impossible as absurd; and his eccentricity is well recognized by the congregation, who regard everything said from the pulpit as irrelevant. Finally, the Vicar (like the only other really "fantastic" character in the book, Mr. Todd) is exceptional in the "real" world of the novel whereas the other characters, though they may be amusing in varying degrees, are credible. Those of *Decline and Fall* are not. Thus, *A Handful of Dust* is a **satire** in which the implied standard of behavior, identical with traditional ethical values, is suggested by its opposite. The novel, then, is not farcical, but ironic; that is, its effect, as we shall see later, depends on a reversal of what is expected. But rather than tragic **irony**, which reveals to us that man cannot escape his destiny, it exemplifies comic **irony**, which reveals to us the extent of man's folly by showing it as ridiculous, even when not "funny."

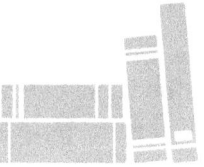

# A HANDFUL OF DUST

## TEXTUAL ANALYSIS

### CHAPTER 3

#### EFFECT AND POINT OF VIEW

The titles of the chapters are meaningful authorial comments on the action of each chapter, as well as indicative of the interrelationship of all chapters. In the case of Chapter Three, the title is an ironic comment on the action which serves to increase the effect of the **irony** that the chapter attains. Another element of technique called point of view also intensifies the author's intended effect. As was indicated in the discussion of *Decline and Fall* (p. 16), the technical term point of view does not refer to the author's general attitude (as, for instance, when we say he has a comic "viewpoint"). Rather, it means specifically the angle of narration, that angle from which the story is told. Now, you may remember, there are three basic points of view, employed in various combinations but distinguishable from one another. One is called the first person because the narrator in that case is the grammatical first person, "I." Another kind is in the third person grammatically, but is called the single or restricted consciousness because everything the reader learns comes through the consciousness of a single, usually central character in the narrative. The third type of point of view, also in the third grammatical person, is the so-called omniscient author. Here the narrator is identical with the author, who addresses the reader directly, and since, so far as his characters are concerned, he is like God - omniscient, or all-knowing - the author can move his characters around at will. He is able, without disturbing the pattern of the narrative, to present characters in different places simultaneously. The most important advantage that this simultaneity gives the author who uses the omniscient point of view is the opportunity to employ contrast. Waugh's major structural device is that of contrast, by means of which he can make implied comparisons and thereby indicate the significance of any section. In addition to the immediate ironic effect which contrast produces, we can also note in Chapter Three an effect of objectivity, even coldness, in the tone of the narration, which adds to the pathos of the whole. Thus the omniscient point of view, we observe, is one of the most effective elements of technique for the author's purpose.

## POINT OF VIEW AND CHARACTER

It is possible to mingle the several kinds of point of view when it is appropriate to the author's purpose and does not destroy the illusion of verisimilitude which all fiction aims at and on which its ultimate effect depends. So the omniscient author may now and then momentarily slip into a character's consciousness and allow us to see things from that character's restricted angle of vision. Waugh does this most often with Tony. When this happens we are getting, so to speak, an interior point of view from which we may directly infer a character's motives. But this is only temporary, and we quickly shift back to the exterior view of the characters, again learning about their motives from their words and actions rather than from participating in their thoughts. The reason for this is that only by such an exterior view can the author's satirical purpose be effected; too much participation in the characters' interior reactions would simply distract the reader. For instance, it is not necessary to, and would even detract from, the single shocking effect that the author aims at, to participate for an instant in Brenda's consciousness. On the contrary, the effect is more powerful when we, with Jock, view objectively the horrible results of Brenda's loss of ordinary human affection and her almost insane obsession with the worthless Beaver. This objective view of her inhumanity accomplishes the author's ultimately satiric purpose - to reveal the extent of human folly - better than any other means he might employ.

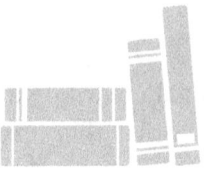

# A HANDFUL OF DUST

## TEXTUAL ANALYSIS

## CHAPTER 4

### ECONOMY AND IMAGERY

One of the major characteristics of Evelyn Waugh's writing has been his preoccupation with style; and critics attempting to describe his style most often note its economy. The quality of a writer's style, including as it does all the elements of his technique, is difficult to assess, but it depends to an important extent on his **diction**; that is, his manner of choosing and putting together the words he uses. In Waugh's style, the most notable quality of his **diction** is its concentration: with a few carefully selected words, he conveys his meaning by implication. In organizing his words into sentences (at least in his "early" style up to *Brideshead Revisited* and to some extent later), the characteristic form is still simple and direct, with few similes and metaphors, and with a restricted use of **imagery**. But, as we have noted in our previous examination of *Decline and Fall*, it is not merely the kinds of words and the way he uses them that contribute to his economy of style; it is a matter also of what he leaves out or implies, and of the careful selection of only what is necessary to the attainment of the intended effect. Chapter Four is an excellent illustration of such economical selection. We recall that Hetton represented those values Tony cherished as well as the dreamworld of gentility he lived in, a direct contrast to the pretension and the ugliness of Beaver's world. In this part of the narrative another contrast is clearly intended; and the terms of the basis contrast are the terms of the story's structure. Waugh clearly reveals his hero's innocence and decency by having him attribute honest motives to everyone else in the face of contrary evidence. Thus, omitting all extraneous material, the author sharply and economically contrasts Tony's foolish but genuine nobility and generosity with the selfishness and dishonesty of those around him.

There is also in this chapter a limited but effective use of **imagery**. The two major images, in the three sections of this chapter, both recall the contrast between the past world of order and certitude that Tony had lived in and his present condition. These images, as well as all the events, even the seemingly incidental ones, are seen in perspective to contribute to the total impression of the whole chapter - the contrast between the past illusions represented by English Gothic and the recognition of the truth that comes with disillusionment.

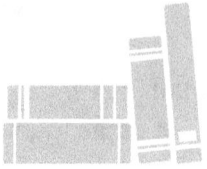

# A HANDFUL OF DUST

## TEXTUAL ANALYSIS

## CHAPTER 5

### THE TWO CITIES

Frank Kermode in his essay, "Mr. Waugh's Cities," points out Waugh's very real tendency in his writings generally to identify the "Catholic City" (of Faith) with a secular order of reason, clarity, and beauty - in fact, Kermode might have added, even with the West, or Western Europe alone. The critic then observes that in Waugh's writings the Great House becomes a "type" - a symbolic representation - of the Catholic City, and, like Hetton, must be defended against barbarism. This observation is quite valid, but its application to the image of the City in the case of *A Handful of Dust* appears too restrictive. That is, the image has a more universal significance here and is not restricted to an identification of Hetton with the traditional order of Catholicism. The image, itself, is derived ultimately from the famous antithesis between the City of God and the City of Man in St. Augustine's great work, *The City of God* - representing the opposition between the permanence and immutability of spiritual values and the transience and mutability of all values based on worldliness of any kind. Now, it is clear that Hetton represents to Tony the ideals associated with such eternal values; but Hetton is also a material possession, and everything in his mind has value as connected with this possession (even his own wife and child). It is finally the exclusive preoccupation with this worldly possession that destroys him; for in seeking another worldly substitute for the secular ideal of Hetton, he is merely fleeing from one dreamworld of illusion to another. And when Tony's last disillusionment comes, he declares that in the wilderness he has learned that there is no City - there is no permanence in worldly things, including even the joy of wife or child. Thus Waugh, through this Hetton-City image and the parallels to it throughout the narrative, creates an implicit standard by which the behavior of all his characters is measured. Beautifully balanced against this image of illusion is Tony's young shipboard acquaintance, Therese de Vitre, a very model of subservience to a traditional, specifically Catholic and aristocratic order of things (which is another illusion of permanence), who ironically rejects Tony because he violates her code of behavior. And thereby Waugh's **satire** is completely controlled and coherent, ridiculing the blindness of humanity to the eternal spiritual values that it seeks in the temporal and worldly City.

## POINT OF VIEW AND CONTRAST

As previously noted, Waugh uses the point of view of omniscient author because it allows him the most latitude in shifting from character to character and place to place without disturbing the reader's sense of verisimilitude. This is in accord with the basic principle of construction in the narrative as a whole, the principle of contrast. The shift back and forth between Tony in the jungle and Brenda in London, both in a state of isolation, reinforces the **theme** of a search for the City (for something permanent in the midst of flux). This whole pattern of ironic parallels culminates with the perfectly appropriate Chapter finale, Tony's vision of the City, an illusion (like Hetton) that does not bring him actual death, but leads him toward a living death.

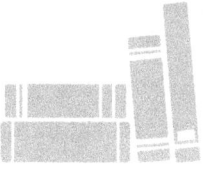

# A HANDFUL OF DUST

## TEXTUAL ANALYSIS

## CHAPTER 6

### Satire and the Absurd

In his excellent study, *The Satiric Art of Evelyn Waugh*, Mr. James F. Carens places the characters of Waugh's novels in three categories. The first is that of the naifs, the innocent, usually central characters whose unworldliness shows up the worldliness and corruption of others - much as do Voltaire's *Candide* and Mark Twain's *Huckleberry Finn*. Generally, these characters are the central figures of Waugh's early satires, like *Decline and Fall* and *Vile Bodies*, and are so naive as to be believable only on the level of farce-fantasy. Though Tony, to some extent, fits into this category, the essential difference is that his innocence is qualified in a way that makes him a new development of the naif. The second category is the associates of the naifs; not farcical caricatures of innocence, they are generally upper-class types like Brenda Last and John Beaver. Carens' third category involves grotesques, who are usually lower-class and have such exaggerated characteristics that they are indeed farcical caricatures. The grotesques are again most prevalent in the earlier satires, though they appear throughout Waugh's novels. The interesting point about Carens' list is that he includes in all three categories only two of the characters from *A Handful of Dust*, and these are the two mentioned in the class of associates, Brenda Last and John Beaver. Tony Last, of course, is a version of the naif in his deluded faith in Brenda, but he is an entirely credible character, not a farcical caricature. But the most significant omission is from the list of grotesques; that is, of at least two characters in the novel, the Hetton Vicar and Mr. Todd. Dr. Messinger is a possible third omission, a borderline case who is close to farcical caricature but still quite credible. The Hetton Vicar figures only marginally in the narrative, but he does embody some idiosyncratic, provincially traditional attitudes redolent of the "white man's burden" and the "divinity" of the British Empire. Dr. Messinger and Mr. Todd, however, are prime contributors to the story line. The last of the three is a curious novelistic construction, a somewhat farcical creation imbued with terrifying overtones of **realism**. What is the nature of Mr. Todd's reality? His demoniacal character is so emphatic that the reader is torn between laughter and horror.

The basic distinction between credible and farcical characters is whether we can believe the characters are possible in the real world, which the novel presumably represents, rather than the fantastic world of farce. In other words, all **satire** is not necessarily farce, and in *A Handful of Dust*, Waugh, though still ridiculing man's folly, is doing it, in terms of plot and character, in a manner closer to the traditional level of **realism** rather than to his earlier level of fantasy. Both central figures in *A Handful of Dust*, Tony and Brenda Last, are entirely credible representations of actual persons, and we learn just enough about them - without the author's resorting to lengthy analyses of motive - to accept their existence, and no more. The question that arises, however, with regard to the Vicar and Mr. Todd, is whether they are credible on the same level of reality or whether they are "fantastic" characters like the grotesques, who do not belong in the same narrative. With regard to the Vicar, it has already been observed that though he is unquestionably considered eccentric, his vagaries are literally possible, and in fact are so notable to Tony's family, for instance, as to be regarded by them as exceptional. Mr. Todd is a more difficult case, and he is significant because of his relationship to the whole idea of **satire** in this novel. That is, Mr. Todd is possible in reality, unlike the farcical grotesques in some of the other novels (and he is in fact modeled on a character Waugh actually met on a jungle plantation under similar circumstances). We do not need to be convinced of his motives because he is clearly insane; but the form that his insanity takes is absurd; that is, it is so far removed from ordinary human experience, while at the same time not beyond the realm of possibility, that if is ridiculous. Thus, Mr. Todd's absurdity is the final expression of the basic **irony** of the **satire**: for irony is the reverse of something intended or expected; and that Tony, attempting to escape from the world in which his lifelong assumptions and certainties have failed him, should be brought, instead of to a tragic end, to a living death, is completely absurd and perfectly ironic.

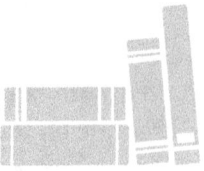

# A HANDFUL OF DUST

## TEXTUAL ANALYSIS

### CHAPTER 7

> A FINAL IRONY

As we have seen, *A Handful of Dust* though a **satire**, is not a farce, as Waugh's **satires** up to this point have been. It is, rather, an example of comic **irony**, which can be most easily understood as the opposite of tragic irony. The latter is a reversal of fortune in which the hero, as Aristotle put it, "suffers a misfortune greater than deserved." Since comic **irony** is the opposite, it must be comic not merely because it reveals the ridiculous aspect of human nature, or has a "happy ending," but essentially because the hero's suffering is not greater than deserved. In Tony's case this might not at first seem appropriate. The sorrow of the death of his son would certainly appear undeserved, but this suffering is the result of an accident, neither deserved nor undeserved, and simply contributes to the misfortune that the hero does bring on himself; for Tony, in his obsession with Hetton, so blinds himself to his wife's growing boredom and frustration, and later so deludes himself in his search for a City that he dooms himself to a living death. The fact is that, in the basic sense of the word, Tony is a fool; and his folly is the universal human assumption that what is ephemeral and mutable is changeless and eternal. Thus the standard by which Waugh holds Tony's delusion up to ridicule is essentially a religious one, implicit throughout the narrative, but clearly indicated throughout by the ironic contrasts. And appropriately enough, this ironic **satire** is concluded with a final note of **irony**, for Tony's young cousin Teddy hopes that he will be able one day to restore Hetton to the "glory" he imagines it had when Tony lived. This accession sets in motion another possible cycle of self-delusion and isolation.

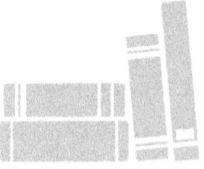

# BRIDESHEAD REVISITED

## PROLOGUE

### POINT OF VIEW

The most immediately important element of technique in the Prologue is what is called point of view. As we have seen in our examination of Waugh's earlier work, this is not the author's general attitude toward his material, as when we say that the author has a "tragic viewpoint" or a "comic viewpoint." Rather, it is a technical term, having to do with the way the writer presents his narrative; that is, with his angle of narration. The "rule," if it may be so called, by which the writer determines which angle of narration to use in any particular narrative is simply to use that point of view that will be most effective for his purpose. (This seems so obvious that we forget that it is possible for a writer to use a less effective point of view than one which would best accomplish his intention.) For *Brideshead Revisited*, Waugh has clearly chosen the first person point of view because the story is intended to be a reminiscence of past experience. This choice has several significant results, but the primary result of the use of the "I" narrator (and central figure) is that throughout the story the reader is limited only to what the narrator can know or learn. In short, the reader sees the story entirely through the consciousness of the "I" narrator.

Now, it is notable that of all his writings, this is the only instance in which Waugh uses this point of view. In his other narratives, he employs the so-called omniscient author, a form of third-person narration in which the author, as narrator, tells the reader all about his characters and, in some cases, things that the characters themselves cannot know. In all the earlier **satires** preceding *Brideshead Revisited* this was the best angle of narration for the purpose, since by using it the author could reveal as much as was necessary of his characters' motives to effect his **satire**, and no more. He could indicate motives through actions, and thus let them speak for themselves, without the necessity of his exploring motivation. But the moment Waugh chose the first-person narrator, he was faced with the problem of the reader's learning about the motivations of the other characters through the narrator alone; and since the significance of the whole narrative ultimately depends on motivation, the narrator, himself, must represent the motives of the other characters or the narrative will fail. And, in fact, there is a general opinion among critics that, for this very reason, *Brideshead Revisited* ultimately does fail to accomplish fully the author's purpose. The justice of this judgment, however, can only be determined after an examination of the whole narrative.

There are some immediate results of the use of the "I" narrator apparent in the Prologue. Most important is that the picture of Platoon Commander Hooper is little more than a caricature, unrelieved by any sense of an older man's (the narrator's) compassion. This fact suggests that the narrator is biased, and so it is possible that the validity of his report of his experience is questionable. But of course, the main purpose of the Prologue is to initiate the reminiscence, and the first-person narrator is appropriate to the purpose.

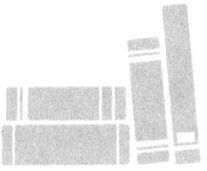

# BRIDESHEAD REVISITED

## TEXTUAL ANALYSIS

## BOOK I

### CHAPTER 1

#### Et in Arcadia Ego

Before examining the body of the novel, it is worth noting the motto on the title page of Book One. Latin for "I too in Arcady," it refers to the name in classical poetry for the place of ideal pastoral peace and beauty, where man is in harmony with his (usually natural) surroundings. It is also an unreal world of refuge from the ugliness and corruption of mankind. As suggested in our examination of Waugh's previous work, the search for a refuge from the corruption and harshness of modern life can be considered a dominant **theme** in his fiction.

#### The Nursery and the Great House

More than one critic has observed that two of the major motifs, or recurrent patterns, in the novels of Evelyn Waugh are what can be called the Nursery Motif and the Great House Motif. The first of these refers to the nostalgic attachment of a number of Waugh's heroes or central figures to their childhood, represented by the nursery; an attachment generally taken to mean innocence and immaturity and, along with these traits, a natural inability or unwillingness to deal with reality. The other motif, the Great House, appears in Waugh's work from the very beginning, when in *Decline and Fall* the great Tudor manor-house, King's Thursday, is used to represent values of the past - order, dignity, continuity - that are threatened by a modern nihilistic age. Now both of these motifs are found combined in *Brideshead Revisited*. Sebastian has substituted Nanny for his mother, who represents the Roman Catholic religion from which he is trying to escape. The Great House is, itself, the Arcadia - the dreamworld of harmony and beauty that is a refuge from the reality of life-which in the end proves as illusory an escape from responsibility as the nursery. Thus, even as Waugh has made a conscious opposition between the aristocratic, or snobbish, values of Brideshead and the vulgarities of Hooper, he has also set up within the framework of the narrative a strong counter-symbol (similar to the symbolic value of Hetton in *A Handful of Dust*): the Great House (or past) as the illusory refuge from the reality of the present, a refuge in which it is suicide to dwell.

## CHAPTER 2

### Symbol and Theme

The question of symbolism in Waugh's writing should be approached cautiously. There are symbols deliberately employed in his work, but not so extensively as to form a system or pattern of symbolic structure that would organize the meaning. For example, in a work like James Joyce's *A Portrait of the Artists a*

*Young Man*, everything on the literal (or realistic) level of the narrative has a correspondence on the symbolic level which thereby gives significance to the literal level. Thus it is the symbolism that organizes the meaning. This is not true, to such an extent at least, of Waugh's writing, though he approaches a symbolic system in *A Handful of Dust*. Now, a symbol is a concrete thing - action, person, event - that by association acquires another, abstract significance. The passage in which Charles makes his way through throngs of Sunday Oxford churchgoers on his solitary way to his beloved friend Sebastian portrays such a symbolic event which adds significance to the narrative as a whole. Since the whole narrative of *Brideshead Revisited* eventuates in the conversion of the narrator to the religion he scorns, it is clear that the contrast between Charles and the throng (drawn to the changeless source of all love) has a symbolic meaning that integrates it with the total narrative. That is not to say, however, that all sections of the novel are so integrated and, therefore, equally meaningful; and as can be seen elsewhere, there are sections that, in light of this kind of symbolic significance, are irrelevant.

## CHAPTER 3

### Structure and Satire

In his study of novelists of the twenties called *The Vanishing Hero*, the Irish writer and critic Sean O'Faolain pays tribute to Waugh as a comic genius, but in an incisive analysis of *Brideshead Revisited* he demonstrates that much of the narrative is irrelevant to the **theme** and constitutes what he calls "unessential trappings." Now, it is a moot question whether the modern critical insistence on the "well-made" structure, in which everything not essential to the effect (no matter how delightful or interesting) is excluded, is entirely justified. Thus, for example, the beauty of Oxford and the immature nostalgia for golden days may not be absolutely essential to the **theme** of Charles Ryder's conversion, but they can be considered as contributing to the past Arcadia that is part of the atmosphere of the narrative. This is, at least, pleasurable decoration which contributes to the overall effect. However, there are other parts of the narrative which seem to contribute nothing to the author's purpose, and indeed, appear to act against his intended effect. The extended semicomic duel between Charles and his father is such an instance.

The duel between father and son is clearly in a different category from the passage in the previous chapter in which Charles moves through the Sunday morning throngs on his way to Sebastian's. This earlier passage, as we have seen, has a symbolic significance related to the **theme** and, in this light, it can be seen as essential to, or at least integrated with, the narrative. This is clearly not the case with the whole section on Charles' father, which is rather a comic interlude that is essentially satiric. The senior Ryder is very close to a caricature; even though he is portrayed as an eccentric (and is therefore ridiculous by the standards of the real world - that is, the realistic world of the novel), he is so close to the level of farce that he strikes a false note in this nonfarcical narrative of romantic reminiscence. Another character who, in later passages, comes close to the same farcical level is Rex Mottram. There are some other instances which also move too close to farce for the narrative of which they are a part, but the foregoing suffices to illustrate the point. Waugh in this novel is using some of the methods of his earlier satiric writing, attempting to adapt them to the purpose of what has been called the "realistic romance" of *Brideshead Revisited*; but in those instances where the adaptation is incomplete, the result is not mere excessive decoration, but distortion of the basic narrative.

## CHAPTER 4

### Theme and Characterization

An author's division of his novel into parts - books, chapters, etc. - is usually purposeful, with each division acting as a unit in the progressive development of his **theme**. Most often these units are in a chronological sequence, though often within this sequence there are flashbacks (movements back in time, generally in someone's thoughts of the past) and even, more rarely, flash-forwards (anticipations of the future that of course depend on the knowledge of the narrator). In the case of *Brideshead Revisited*, with the narrator reminiscing about the past, there is such a general chronological sequence, with now and then a flashback or flash-forward to amplify the narrative. But the narrator doesn't give away anything that might reduce the suspense; instead, he increases it so the general movement is chronological, with each chapter-unit serving a function. Chapter Four is a good illustration of this function. Up till now, we have had only hints about Sebastian's family that have served to rouse our curiosity. Chapter Four satisfies our curiosity to some extent, but also rouses it further on the subject of their religion. Thus we have here the first explicit introduction of the **theme** which has to do generally with Catholicism. The full comprehension of the **theme**, however, depends on our understanding of the characters, that is, on the narrator's revelations of their motives. It is therefore essential that their motives be credible to the reader - to all readers, not just to Catholics - and that they should therefore be represented as universally valid human motives, common to everyone. But as a matter of fact, in this chapter Waugh represents his characters' motives as depending on some secret understanding of religion, shared by initiates but baffling to the non-initiates like Charles (and even, it might be added, to some Catholic readers!). Of course, it is indicated that the traditional, but not exclusive, Catholic insistence on the submission to God's will, and the consequent necessity to conform to a system of values different from those of "the world," is a source of difficulty for someone like Sebastian. This is perfectly comprehensible to any reader, whatever his beliefs. But that is precisely what is not the case with Sebastian, as the author presents him. Sebastian is presumably rebelling against his mother's possessiveness, but why this possessiveness should necessarily depend on her Catholic faith is never made clear. There may be other credible reasons for Sebastian's or, for that matter, Lord Marchmain's actions, but this possibility is completely obscured by the author's attempt to attribute some mysterious and indefinable influence to their religion. This attempt, continued throughout the narrative, weakens the credibility of the characters on whom the process of the hero's conversion depends and ultimately undermines the effective presentation of his theme.

## CHAPTER 5

### Charles the Naif

In his excellent study *The Satiric Art of Evelyn Waugh*, James F. Carens puts Waugh's characters into three general categories. The first of these he calls the naifs, or innocents, who are usually the heroes, or at least central figures, like Paul Pennyfeather in *Decline and Fall* and Tony Last in *A Handful of Dust*. They are usually likeable and, as the name indicates, innocent of the corruptions of the world they inhabit, thereby providing a contrast which the author employs to satirize those corruptions. It is a classic pattern in **satire**, and it is one of the methods adapted by the satirist Waugh to the form of "realistic romance" he created in *Brideshead Revisited*. Charles clearly belongs in the category of the innocent. He is, despite his surface sophistication, quite young and even ignorant of much of the world, romantic and readily impressed, especially by the glamor of the aristocratic Flytes. But there is a crucial difference between the function of the central figure's naivete in the earlier **satires** and in *Brideshead Revisited*. For here, Charles does not act as a foil or contrast to the corrupt world around him (though in juxtaposition to Sebastian's friend Anthony Blanche he might incidentally serve as such); rather his function in the narrative is to act as the central figure in the process of discovering a "reality" that he was previously ignorant of - a process that makes up the plot of the novel. It is in this sense mainly, in his innocence of the "truth" that the novel is intended to arrive at, that he is a naif. Thus, the first-person narrator reconstructs the past through his reminiscence, in such a manner that the stages of discovery become the stages of development in the narrative; and what the narrator has already learned is withheld, so to speak, in order to involve the reader in the gradual discovery.

However, one of the inherent dangers that the author using such a method must be alert to is the temptation to project back upon the narrator, as he was then, any feelings, ideas, or attitudes that he could only properly have later. Waugh succumbs to this temptation when he shows Charles reading the posthumous collection of Lady Marchmain's brother and reflecting on it from his youthful and ignorant vantage point, while at the same time referring to Hooper, with whom he is not yet acquainted. It is clear that the flaw here is Waugh's abandonment of technique for the sake of a sermon that expresses (and not too clearly) his own prejudices and that has no possible validity as an expression of opinion by Charles the naif. Thus Waugh destroys the validity of his narrator, whose experience of the process of discovery, leading to his conversion, is the ostensible purpose of the novel.

## CHAPTER 6

### Charles the Gourmet

It is obvious that the hero, like his author, is a gourmet who knows and appreciates good food and wine. This is not the only place in his writings where Waugh makes such appreciation a kind of index of the true gentleman; he does this, for instance, in talking about his hero, Paul Pennyfeather, in *Decline and Fall*. In every instance of this kind, of course, there is an implicit snobbery: those who have the money and leisure to acquire such tastes, as well as the intelligence to recognize their true significance, must be superior to the common run of mankind. All of this is present in this book; but nowhere else in Waugh's work is there such a deliberate counterpoint - like two musical **themes** set in juxtaposition, one against the other - between the initiate (Charles), who is aware of the true values, and the ignoramus (Rex), who is not. The question naturally arises as to the function of this contrast in the narrative.

One possibility (though we can probably never be quite sure exactly what Waugh is trying to do in this section) is that the narrator's obvious feelings of superiority toward Rex derive primarily from his feelings of jealousy. The reader remembers Sebastian's comments, long ago, about the great spiritual and physical closeness between him and his sister, and the narrator's sudden, startled recognition of this fact. Now that Sebastian has gotten started on his route downhill to drunkenness and disintegration, what could be more emotionally logical than for the narrator to experience intense feelings of closeness and concern for Julia? He cannot easily tear out of himself a family, a life style, which had become implanted to some degree within him.

Another function of the contrast between Charles and Rex may also be possible. The values involved are associated with the purely sensual pleasure of eating. However, they are automatically converted by the narrator into social values, resulting in the recognition of his superiority. Moreover, his superior perception includes a kind of mystical recognition of the ultimate significance of the pleasure of food. Now, it is possible that all this was intended to reveal the narrator's appreciation of the true good in creation, in contrast to Mottram's lack of such appreciation, and to thereby establish the authority of the narrator when it came to the recognition of higher spiritual truth. But this is by no means clear to the reader, and since the total implication seems that of pure and simple snobbery, based on the standards of a private and rather exclusive club, the reader's belief in the narrator's judgment (and the author's artistic objectivity) may be seriously impaired.

## CHAPTERS 7, 8

### The Key to Sebastian

These last two chapters of Book One form a unit, dealing successively with Julia and Sebastian, and thus completing the pictures of the two characters most important to the central figure just at the point in the narrative before a time lapse of ten years. Though all of the subsidiary relationships have been well established, most of Book One has been taken up with the relationship of Charles and Sebastian and, in fact, has been preoccupied with Sebastian. Charles meets Julia very early in the narrative, but sees her intermittently, and we learn almost nothing of her motives; she appears hard and somewhat shallow.

Chapter Seven serves two functions in the development of the narrative: it contributes to the primitive element of suspense, and it prepares us for the later change in Julia by a flash-forward, or movement ahead in time. Because of the love relationship our interest is further engaged; and in addition, we are readier than we might otherwise be to overlook the jump in time sequence which requires the telescoping of ten years into a few paragraphs. More important to the whole narrative, however, is the recounting of Julia's personal history, partly through the narrator's reconstruction and partly through her own (later) account. This provides us with a clear picture of her development.

We are satisfied that she is not so shallow as she first appeared, and also not quite so indifferent to her family's religion, though she is apparently free from the kind of religious agony that Sebastian suffers. By contrast, Sebastian's battle with his private demons is the subject of the concluding chapter of Book One, where Charles has the last encounter with him. And the contrast points up again the weakness of the whole narrative, which depends for its ultimate significance on the credibility of the leading characters' religious experiences and the difficulties that their beliefs cause them. Julia's motives, this far, are recognizable and universal and thus credible. But again, when we come to the attempt to understand Sebastian, we find the same kind of hints and speculations that have been used earlier to characterize him. The motivation, and thus the characterization, of Sebastian is incomplete; and since it is expressed in terms of a religious conflict, which is likewise obscure, it serves not to clarify but rather to obscure the theme.

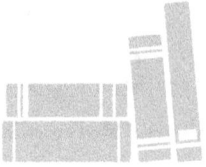

# BRIDESHEAD REVISITED

## TEXTUAL ANALYSIS

## BOOK II

### CHAPTERS 1-3

#### The Time Dimension and Character

In popular parlance, time in Einstein's theory is the "fourth dimension," but in function it is one of three - the other two being place and action. These three are often considered to be the so-called Unities (wrongly ascribed to Aristotle who, in his *Poetics*, did consider Unity of Action and did mention time). There is no doubt that one of the major problems for the novelist to deal with is the passage of time. It may be dealt with in many ways, depending on the novelist's purpose. For example, in his famous novel *The Scarlet Letter*, Nathaniel Hawthorne handles the problem of time rather indirectly. That is, he concentrates almost solely on the development of his characters' inner lives - their motivations - and alludes now and then quite casually to the passage of time. The reader is conscious, then, of years elapsing but hardly notices their passing. On the other hand, the novelist may meet the problem head-on, so to speak, and deal with it directly, as Waugh does here. This is necessarily imposed on him, of course, by his first-person narrator who is recalling the past. Since there is a lapse of ten years, and then of two, between sections - a lapse required by the story - the writer must manage the reminiscence so that the total unified impression is not lost and the reader is not jarred out of the illusion by jumping from one point in time to the next.

Moreover, and more important, the author must make sure that any changes, especially in character, that take place during the time lapses are clearly accounted for. Aside from Charles, the central character in Book Two is Julia, and it is with the development of Julia's motivation that the latter part of the narrative is largely concerned. This development, however - or rather, the reader's knowledge of this development - reaches back into the earlier parts of the narrative, though at first, we see her indistinctly and know her, as Charles does, only in a distorted way. Gradually, her image becomes more distinct, until the narrator turns directly to her and anticipates her future development by referring to her as she is after the ten-year lapse. The demand that this places on the writer is to account for her motivation in such a way that any change is credible to the reader. This is done first by reviewing the events of her life up to the point of her reacquaintance with Charles, thus providing the reader with some explanation for changes in her attitudes and behavior.

There are several notes sounded, however, that foretell another change, one that becomes increasingly important to the whole narrative. These are the transparently obvious hints that Julia's conscience is troubled; and so it does not surprise us greatly when she reacts hysterically. Nevertheless, the crucial fact here is that between the end of her self-revelation and the revelation by the narrator of her stirring religious scruples, there are two years quickly glossed over in the narrative that, so far as Julia's inner life is concerned, are unaccounted for. Thus the telescoping of time has allowed the narrator to evade, except for a few hints, a developing change in motivation that is crucial to the coming climax.

## CHAPTER 4

### Theme and Imagery

There are several instances in next to the last chapter of the kind of **imagery** that Waugh uses throughout the narrative, often as a rhetorical device to intensify the effect, but not always connected with the overall **theme**. In the present instances, however, the images are directly expressive of the **theme** and are employed at the point where the narrative is reaching its **climax**. The **theme** that is implied by these images, once the action is completed, is obvious; but the reason for using the **imagery** (aside from the usual function of making the idea concrete and so more vivid) is instructive with reference to the purpose and method of the whole narrative. For example, of the several images employed, one group is a metaphorical expression of the idea common to religious literature that human love is but an adumbration or shadowing forth of the love of God. Another image, of the horse, clearly implies Charles' recognition of his refusal so far to consider the claims of revealed religion on their own merits. And the final image, of a gathering avalanche (of faith) that will sweep all (doubt) away, is an unequivocal indication that Charles is on the brink of assent. Now, the important fact to note about this use of **imagery** is that it is the only indication of the change taking place in the narrator, who is otherwise completely noncommittal about the effect on him of the events in which he participates. In short, **imagery** is substituted for any explicit examination of his own motives on the part of the narrator, thereby leaving a gap in the development of the motivation central to the whole narrative, and thus seriously impairing the credibility of the whole.

## CHAPTER 5

### Apologetics and Didactics

In his study of Waugh's works in *The Satiric Art of Evelyn Waugh*, James F. Carens maintains that *Brideshead Revisited* is not a work of apologetics (a work defending the truth of Christian religion, as an apologia or apology for its beliefs). He supports his argument by citing the Flyte family's confusion about points of Catholic doctrine, maintaining that the confusion is used to further characterize Charles, who is scoffing at what by now he half believes. Carens' observation is all very well and good, but more central points in this part of the novel must escape Carens' interpretation. It is certain beyond doubt that much in the **climax** of the narrative, if not apologetics (in the sense of a systematic defense of dogma) is at least **didactic**; that is, it attempts to teach a lesson that is not only the truth of Christianity but the unique truth of Catholicism. To deny this is to misrepresent the clear intention present in the **theme** of conversion as the basis of the whole narrative. But it is possible to misunderstand the intention because of the manner in which it is represented, namely by implication. Nowhere does the narrator explicitly state that the events in which he participates provide him with irrefutable evidence for the religion he eventually embraces. Not that he would be concerned at this moment logically to consider the historic claims of Catholicism; what he is affected by is the powerful influence of this religion on the lives of others who embrace it, especially the woman he loves. But where is there any indication that Julia's decision is a universally valid experience of God's grace? The narrator has revealed next to nothing about Julia's motives, aside from a few indications of her troubled conscience. There has been no internal struggle or resolution that carries with it the conviction that her decision is a genuine recognition of Divine Will - in fact, it appears more likely to be a natural emotional reaction. Of course, we see only what Charles sees, and to him he power of faith is exemplified in Lord Marchmain's conversion; but the reader sees no reason to assume that it is any better than another such witness to God's grace. For the reader sees Charles from the outside, and the sole indication of his thoughts is the **imagery** that is carried over from the previous chapter. This image, of the avalanche of faith that sweeps away all doubts, is a very effective and poetic expression of the idea of conversion; but this does not gainsay the fact that it is used as a substitute for a complete revelation of motives that alone would make the process of conversion, which is the **theme** of the narrative, credible to the reader as a universal human experience, regardless of race, creed, or social status. Thus, the narrative, weakened by evasion and confusion, finally fails to carry the conviction necessary to express the **theme**; and the novel as a whole, despite its many brilliancies, must be counted an artistic failure.

## EPILOGUE

### Postscript

The final **imagery** of the narrative, it should be noted, returns to the image of the Great House. Even in ruins, amidst the desolation of the modern world, it harbors the light of faith. It is a lovely poetic image, but it identifies a universal faith with a social system that is far from universal, and thereby reveals the ultimate failure of the novel. As Sean O'Faolain (a Catholic) put it in his essay on Waugh in *The Vanishing Hero*, instead of universalizing his **theme** of conversion, Waugh institutionalized it. The institution, glamorous and romantic though it may be, cannot represent universal human experience. It might well be an appropriate conclusion to observe that the final image of the Great House in ruins is, unbeknownst to the author, the last word on *Brideshead Revisited*.

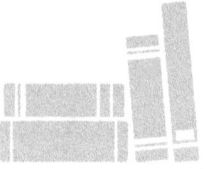

# THE LOVED ONE

## TEXTUAL ANALYSIS

### CHAPTER 1

| Satire and Snobbery

One of the recurrent charges that Evelyn Waugh faced, and at times encouraged, during his lifetime was that of snobbery. Since his heroes, or central figures, were invariably upper-class Englishmen, and his satiric caricatures or grotesques often (but not invariably) lower-class people, there was some reason for this charge. In addition, his romantic treatment of the British aristocracy in *Brideshead Revisited* - his most popular work, though far from his best - furthered the impression that the standard, or norm, by which he judged and ridiculed the objects of his **satire** must necessarily be that of an upper-class English snob. The trouble with this kind of assumption is that it can distort the intention of Waugh's better work and obscure, for example, the brilliant **satire** of the opening chapter of *The Loved One* - a work often regarded as the most artistically perfect of all his satires. Waugh's use of the classic image of the English outpost of civilization among the barbarians is one of many such instances which suggest that supposedly civilized people are just as barbaric as uncivilized ones. We have already seen this suggested in *A Handful of Dust*, where Waugh parallels life in London and the South American jungle. At the opening of *The Loved One*, it seems that we have an island of gentility amidst the surrounding barbarism and that this gentility-the traditions of a chivalric code of behavior - will be the satiric norm for the whole narrative. But then we discover that the gentility is only a pose, and that the English colony apes the social behavior of the English aristocracy purely for the sake of the prestige and economic advantage it will bring.

Furthermore, though it is not apparent at first, the narrative hero (in the sense of central figure, not of personal heroism), Dennis Barlow, even though he is aware of the values of such a traditional code, is completely self-centered and unscrupulous. He is, in fact, a **satire** on Waugh's part of "art for art's sake" morality. The norm for this **satire** is not that of upper-class English snobbery; indeed, that snobbery is itself satirized as a fraud from the vantage point of a more universal standard that begins to emerge as the narrative progresses.

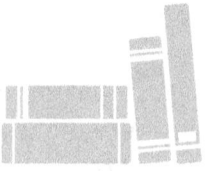

# THE LOVED ONE

## TEXTUAL ANALYSIS

## CHAPTER 2

### POINT OF VIEW

Like all his fiction, with the one exception of *Brideshead Revisited* (which is a first-person narrative), *The Loved One* uses the narrative point-of-view of the so-called omniscient author. (For previous discussions of the technique of point of view, see pages 16, 30, and 38.) The use, in this narrative, of the third-person omniscient narrator, aside from the advantages of mobility, has to do with character development, or the representation of motives. With the omniscient point of view, the author can choose when, and to what extent, to reveal the motivation of his characters; he can thus limit the interior revelation to what he considers necessary for his effect. And since in the case of Evelyn Waugh the intended effect is almost always satiric, he is more concerned with people's actions than with their motives; that is, in the classic mode of **satire**, he is concerned with the exterior and social rather than with the interior and psychological. Thus we learn just enough about Dennis Barlow to make him acceptable, or credible to us. We learn enough to allow him to serve his function in the narrative. Similarly we have learned only so much as was needed about Sir Francis, who is hardly a "real" person at all, but simply a character whose function defines him. The point-of-view of the omniscient author is frequently more appropriate to the purpose of the author - the purpose of **satire** - than any other kind.

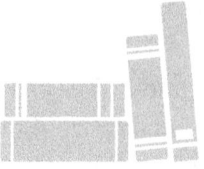

# THE LOVED ONE

## TEXTUAL ANALYSIS

## CHAPTER 3

### THE RELIGION OF DEATH

Mr. Christopher Hollis, in his excellent study of Evelyn Waugh (*Writers and Their Works Series*, No. 46), says that *The Loved One* is essentially the most serious and religious of all of Waugh's works. He goes on to point out that it is a study, in fantasy form, of the modern attitude toward death, a basically irreligious attitude, since the last consideration is the Christian belief in the immortality of the soul. Thus, all the values of Christianity are inverted, and what is of supreme importance in traditional Christian belief is of least importance in the religion of death practiced at Whispering Glades, and vice versa. Therefore the very idea of immortality is materialized, or reduced to a completely mortal dependence on the material strength of stone and steel. Material success - success in life - is carried over to success in death since one can insure in advance, through financial arrangements, a high place in the pantheon of burial zones: a direct contradiction of the Christian insistence on the supremacy of the spiritual as, in fact, the only measure of eternal success. Further, the crucial fact of death as the irrevocable change of state, which is impassable to the living, is minimized and glossed over with euphemisms. The final touch is the hideous imitation of life in the Slumber Room (a euphemism for funeral parlor wake, or the watch over the body before burial). In the Slumber Room the corpse is preserved in such a way that the agony of death is (by the magic of cosmetics, or art) transfigured into pseudolife; a gruesome **parody** of the Christian tradition of Christ that, in the Gospels, signifies eternal glory. Thus throughout, the religion of death at Whispering Glades is a **parody** of traditional Christian practice and suggests through its reverse the satiric norm of the whole narrative, namely, the universal beliefs and rites of the Catholic (universal) Church.

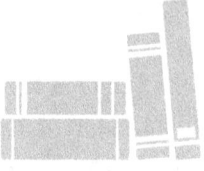

# THE LOVED ONE

## TEXTUAL ANALYSIS

### CHAPTER 4

#### WAUGH'S NAMES

One of the clues to an author's intention, whether it is hidden or overt, is the names he gives to his characters. James Joyce, for example, in his famous novel *A Portrait of the Artist as a Young Man*, names his hero Stephen Dedalus; and when we know that Dedalus is the name of the famous artist-craftsman in Greek mythology, we can safely assume that the hero's name is symbolic, as indeed the whole novel is. Such names are significant because of their associations; but there are other names whose significance is even more obvious. These kinds of names are traditionally associated with satire, and they are often called tag-names, because they are like tags or signs that give away the meaning of the character in the play or novel in which they appear. For example, one of the most famous tag-names is that of a character in Richard Brinsley Sheridan's play, *The Rivals*, one Mrs. Malaprop, who comically misuses the English language. Her name, meaning roughly "inappropriate," has given rise to a word in the English language - malapropism - meaning a misused word. Now, it is clear that tag-names are used to pinpoint the characteristics the author wants to emphasize, but it should also be remembered that such names are invariably an indication that the characters are types. That is, they are representatives of a general class - like jealous husbands, hypocrites, absent-minded professors, and so on - rather than individuals. They do not therefore require any further characterization, for their names have already sufficiently characterized them for their function, which is to represent the aspect of human nature or society that is the satirist's target.

The satirist's target is thus indicated by his characters' names; but more than this, we should not expect his characters to be "real" in the same way as other characters. They are not meant to be complete representations of complex human beings whose motives have to be realistically accounted for; they are meant rather to be appropriate to the manner in which they act or, as Aristotle long ago put it, to "what that kind of person would do in such a situation." So the name Aimee Thanatogenos means "the beloved one born to death" or "of the race of death." It is a tag-name for a character whose motives - to the extent that they are considered at all - are not inconsistent with her actions in a narrative that is on the level of fantasy, or as Waugh says in his little prefatory warning, "nightmare." Mr. Joyboy is the only other character with a tag-name, and he and Aimee, their relationship reeking of perversity, are the only two characters connected with Whispering Glades. Their names heighten the unreal feeling that the author wants to convey in his "nightmare," while Dennis Barlow, a more neutral figure, has a more ordinary name, indicating a stronger connection with reality.

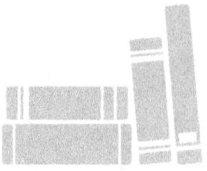

# THE LOVED ONE

## TEXTUAL ANALYSIS

### CHAPTER 5-6

#### DENNIS THE MENACE

These two chapters make apparent what the English critic, Christopher Hollis, in his study of Evelyn Waugh (*Writers and Their Work Series*) remarked about Dennis Barlow. Hollis observed that if we consider him as a real person, he appears to us an entirely repulsive character. And as becomes even more apparent as the narrative unfolds, he is cruel and callous in his attitude toward and treatment of Aimee and is generally heartless and self-centered. Dennis' supposed kindness to Sir Francis Hinsely is merely for self-advantage, since he is eager for the opportunity to find out all about Whispering Glades. And he is fascinated by Aimee as by some kind of curiosity, a product of her culture who will give him material for his poetry. All of this would certainly repel us if, as Hollis says, we considered the character "real." The word if carries the point; Hollis goes on to observe that there is little danger of our considering him as real "in that sense" (the sense of the nonfictional world).

In what sense, then, is he "real"? To answer that question we have to recognize the author's intention in creating the character, which is not merely to present us with a picture of a repulsive character for its own sake. It is obvious that the intention of the work in which the character appears is satiric, and so the significance of the character, his "reality," lies in what he represents. What Dennis represents, and what is being satirized, is what the author considers the complete loss of values that is characteristic of a modern irreligious culture, a loss that leads to the kind of nihilistic delight in decadence and corruption that Dennis evinces, along with a callous disregard for all human feeling. It is this nihilism, ultimately sadistic and destructive, that Waugh is attacking in the character of Dennis, not the character himself. And the final touch by Waugh, the great satiric stylist who reveres and emulates the great artists of the past, is to make Dennis a poet who considers his art more important than the humanity for whom he presumably creates it. This ultimate corruption of the artist is, to the passionately religious author, another aspect of the total corruption of civilization that is the object of his satiric ridicule.

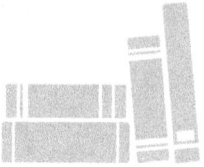

# THE LOVED ONE

## TEXTUAL ANALYSIS

### CHAPTER 7-9

## POOR AIMEE

Considered as a heroine of a realistic novel, Aimee is certainly one of the most pitiable figures in all of literature. But of course, she is not the heroine of a realistic novel; she is a character in a satiric fantasy, and her "reality" is completely limited to and determined by her function in the **satire**. That is, she is a figure who represents something else that is real that the satirist is holding up to ridicule, as in the case of Dennis Barlow. The difference between the two is the difference in their functions in the **satire**; and if Dennis is the nihilistic modern barbarian, Aimee is the victim of that barbarism. Since her name, Aimee Thanatogenos, is a combination of "beloved" and "born of death," she clearly signifies the corruption of human love by the destructive antihuman culture that, fittingly, ends by worshipping death. Aimee, then, is that culture, in its extreme expression; and her suicide is the logical conclusion to her existence.

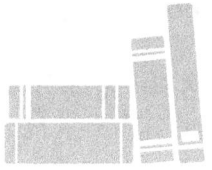

# THE LOVED ONE

## TEXTUAL ANALYSIS

### CHAPTER 10

---

#### SAVAGE INDIGNATION

Among the numerous accusations that Evelyn Waugh endured in his lifetime as one of the major satirists in the English language, a repeated one was cruelty. He was reputedly cruel to children (in his books, that is) as witness the indiscriminate and casually treated death of a child in *Decline and Fall* or the vicious misuse of poor waifs in *Put Out More Flags*, to mention only two examples. No doubt anticipating the outcries of those he described therein as "the squeamish," he prefaced *The Loved One* with a warning to them not to read it since the story was a "nightmare" resulting from his visit to Hollywood, and, therefore, was possibly "somewhat gruesome" from their point of view. This preface sounds rather whimsical, but there is behind it a serious recognition that a number of readers would not understand the intent of the book and could as a result be offended or even sickened by it. Waugh is, in fact, warning them that *The Loved One* is not intended to be a mere joke or "entertainment," but a deliberate and slashing, even savage, attack on modern civilization, especially where, in Waugh's opinion, it is manifested in its most extreme forms - in the United States and, most notably, in Los Angeles. It should be remembered, however, that Dennis is English, not American, and worse than the others in that he is conscious at every moment of the moral values involved in everything he does. But it should be remembered also, and most especially, that Dennis is not to be judged as a real person, but only as a symbol of Waugh's true target which is all of modern civilization; a civilization that has, in his view as an orthodox Christian, deserted all traditional values and has, therefore, inevitably doomed itself to the kind of barbarism evident in the actions of Dennis and Mr. Joyboy.

It is remarked several times in the course of the narrative that Jews and Catholics do not come to Whispering Glades because they have their own burial practices. In other words, the Judeo-Christian tradition is still very much alive in a saving remnant that will preserve the truth, but the majority who comprise the prevailing culture are devotees of a pseudo-religion that is, appropriately, the worship of Death. The point that should be constantly kept in mind, and that is not evident in a work like *The Loved One*, is that Waugh is a deeply religious man and a sensitive artist who is more disturbed than the ordinary person and is, in fact, incensed by what he considers the corruption of the truth. His response is the classic response of the great satirist that has been described by the Latin phrase saeva indignatio, or savage indignation. That is, he is so infuriated that he imaginatively translates his anger into a form so "savage" or outrageous that it will shock others into recognition of the truth. He communicates his anger to the reader in hopes that they will correct the abuse, and, in this way, he is fulfilling the classic function of the satirist - to reform through ridicule.

But to ridicule is ultimately to make a judgment, and to make a judgment some kind of standard is required, some norm by which the deviation can be measured. In this case, it is Waugh's Christian belief, specifically Catholicism, that provides the norm. This norm is implicit in the whole narrative; for the pseudo-religion of Death is a **parody** (a ridiculous imitation) of the traditional belief that is present throughout as a background and as a silent condemnation of the false one. And the final condemnation of the false worship of a "successful" death is that it equates people with animals. Waugh's attack on the false values of modern civilization is completed by his condemnation of another pseudo-religion, the religion of Art. The worship of Art is the motive for Dennis Barlow's inhuman cruelty; and through this character's shocking behavior, Waugh drives home his point that Art as an end in itself is as ultimately inhuman as the religion of Death.

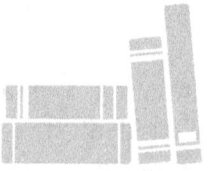

# CHARACTER ANALYSES

Characters are listed alphabetically under the title of the novel in which they appear.

## DECLINE AND FALL

### Margot Beste-Chetwynde

The "heroine," is a realistic rather than farcical character, and in the **satire** functions as a representative of the corrupt aristocracy.

### Peter Beste-Chetwynde

Margot's son is a minor character and, like his mother, is a realistic rather than farcical creation; he figures in the **satire** of the corrupt aristocracy.

### Lady Circumference

The plain-spoken representative of conservative aristocracy, she is a minor character whose only function is farcical.

### Dr. Fagan

He fits the category of a grotesque who functions entirely on the farcical level.

### Captain Edgar Grimes

One of the major grotesques in the farcical action.

### Sir Wilfred Lucas-Dockery

A minor farcical figure.

### Sir Miles Maltravers

A caricature of a self-seeking politician.

### Paul Pennyfeather

The **protagonist**, or central figure of the novel, who functions as a naif whose innocence reveals the corruption of those he encounters. Though he is representative of upper-class gentility, he is not a "realistic" embodiment of the gentlemanly ideal so much as simply the center of the farcical action.

### Sir Solomon Philbrick

A major grotesque character, who is not, however, essential to the farcical action. Rather, as a graduate from the underworld who has assumed the status of "gentry" (knighthood, if not a title), he satirizes the corruption of the aristocratic ideal.

## Mr. Prendergast

A major grotesque character. Like Philbrick, not so essential to the farcical action as he is a means to satirize the chaos of the Church and society at large.

## Dr. Otto Silenus

A minor grotesque, a caricature of the modern architect who hates beauty. He plays no essential part in the farce, but near the end, Silenus explains his theory of life and provides a suggestion for a possible norm of judgment in the total satire.

## Lord Tangent

A minor character.

# A HANDFUL OF DUST

## Jenny Abdul Akbar

A minor comic character.

### Alan (first Name)

A minor figure, he reflects the general indifference of their friends and relatives to Brenda's betrayal of Tony.

### John Beaver

He is a social parasite whose function in the narrative - aside from the ridicule of his pretensions to gentility - is to provide the catalyst for the dissolution of Brenda Last's marriage.

### Mrs. Beaver

Her pretensions to gentility are, like her son's, the object of ridicule; but her main function is to epitomize the character of the group that encourages Brenda to destroy her marriage.

### Therese De Vitre

A minor figure, she is a completely characterized representative of a traditional old-world Catholic code, and functions as a contrast and parallel to Tony's illusory dreamworld.

### Jock Grant-Menzies

He serves the function of a neutral observer through whom both Tony and Brenda are seen.

### Brenda Last

The nominal "heroine," she is a realistic and completely convincing portrait of a weak, shallow woman whose betrayal of her husband is the ultimate result of his blind obsession with family tradition.

### John Andrew Last

Brilliantly drawn, he is Waugh's most successful characterization of a child; his comic precocity adds to the pathos of his parents' separation and his death.

### Tony Last

The **protagonist**, or central figure, of the narrative. A completely realized character whose ideals of honor and decency are inadequate to the demands of reality.

### Marjorie (first Name)

Brenda's sister, she shares the general attitudes of fashionable society.

### Dr. Messinger

He is close to the grotesque type, but nevertheless a credible eccentric character whose function is to reveal Tony's continued blindness to reality.

## Millie

A minor figure, a prostitute.

## Mrs. Rattery

A minor character, she fulfills an important function in heightening the pathos of the child's death, with which Tony's dreamworld begins to crumble.

## Reggie St. Cloud

A minor comic figure.

## Vicar Tendril

A minor figure, but of central importance in establishing the sense of unreality of the dreamworld in which Tony Last lives.

## Mr. Todd

An adaptation of the character-type of the grotesque in Waugh's earlier fantasy-satires, he is a credible maniac whose function is to complete the **irony** of Tony's attempted escape from reality.

## BRIDESHEAD REVISITED

### Anthony Blanche

A minor figure in the plot, he resembles the character-type of the grotesque in earlier satires, but as a sexual deviant is realistically portrayed; and he is an obvious contrast to the charitable Sebastian.

### Cara

A minor character, she is kindly and understanding.

### Brideshead Flyte

Ponderous, literal, and dogmatic in his religion, he is the exact opposite of Sebastian. A major character, especially in his influence on Julia.

### Cordelia Flyte

A major character, she is profoundly devout and charitable.

### Julia Flyte

The heroine, she is, along with Sebastian, one of the two most important, and in her ultimate influence on Charles, the most important of the main characters in the narrative. A sympathetic and appealingly human character, she is more completely revealed than Sebastian. Though in her final actions, since she is seen solely through the eyes of the narrator, her motivation is incompletely exposed.

### Sebastian Flyte

Along with his sister Julia, he is one of the two main characters, but he is less fully explored; and his motivation, though explained to Charles by other characters at various stages, is never completely clear.

### Cousin Jasper

A minor character, he is a comical "stuffed shirt" whose function is to represent the general attitude toward Sebastian.

### Kurt

A minor character, his sole function is to reveal Sebastian's frustrated desire to practice charity.

### Father Mackay

A minor figure, he is a genial unsophisticated man whose simple faith is a contrast to Charles Ryder's scornful disbelief.

### Lady Marchmain

A major character, she is a simple woman in whom great piety and fierce possessiveness combine.

### Lord Marchmain

A major figure, his characterization is inadequate to account for his conversion.

### Rex Mottram

A major character, he is a ruthless social climber whose main function (aside from some ill-conceived **satire** of religious superstition) is to provide Julia with the motive for her affair.

### Boy Mulcaster

A minor character, his moral degeneracy is a reflection of Sebastian's alienation from ordinary society.

### Mrs. Beryl Muspratt

A minor comic character, her only other function is to inspire Bridey's criticism of Julia's affair.

### Nanny

A minor character, she is a representative of traditional belief, but also figures in the narrative as a substitute mother for Sebastian, whose devotion to her, and to his childhood, is a sign of his desire to escape from reality.

## Celia (Mulcaster) Ryder

A brilliantly drawn minor character.

## Charles Ryder

The **protagonist** and first-person narrator of the story. An adaptation of the naif hero, he is "innocent" of the religious belief that he ultimately adopts; and it is the process of his gradual discovery of this belief that forms the basis of the narrative.

## Mr. Ryder

A minor character, he is too close to caricature for the realistic context of the novel, and not only plays no essential part in the narrative but creates a jarring effect detrimental to the tone of the whole.

## Mr. Samgrass

A minor character, his only function in the narrative is to provide information about Sebastian's activities.

# THE LOVED ONE

## Sir Ambrose Abercrombie

A minor character, his sole function, aside from satirizing the snobbery of bogus aristocracy, is to involve Dennis in the funeral and thereby introduce him to Whispering Glades.

## Dennis Barlow

One of the three major characters, he is the center of the narrative and, at the same time, an associate of the heroine, Aimee Thanatogenos.

## Sir Francis Hinsely

A minor character.

## Mr. Joyboy

One of the three major characters, he is the ultimate version of Waugh's type of the grotesque character, while at the same time an associate of Aimee. He represents the complete corruption of the society that supports him.

## Aimee Thanatogenos

Aimee Thanatogenos (a combination meaning "beloved" and, variously, "born of" or "of the race of death"): The "Loved One," she is one of the three major characters; a type of naif, or innocent, whose purity of devotion, in contrast to the corruption of Dennis Barlow and Mr. Joyboy, is a condemnation of them and the society they represent.

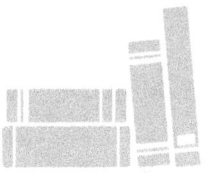

# ESSAY QUESTIONS AND ANSWERS

Below is a model essay of the kind a student might write in response to a topic given in the form of a question. The student should study its construction, noticing its parts: (I) an introductory statement of the topic; (II) a body or central section which elaborates on the statement with illustrations or references to the text; and (III) a conclusion which sums up the argument. The basic divisions, therefore, include at least three paragraphs (often more subdivisions in II). The student should then attempt to compose his own essay, selecting one of the questions following the model essay and elaborating on the points in the outline that provide a basis for the essay. All essay questions refer to matter found in the commentary and analysis of works included in this volume.

Question: How much justification is there for saying that Waugh's characters fall into distinct categories?

Answer: I Introduction: Definition of Terms

    A. It has been maintained that Waugh's characters fall into three main categories - the naif, the associates, and the grotesques. The naif (French, "naive") is the hero or central figure, like Don Quixote or Huck Finn, whose innocence contrasts with and shows up the corruption of those he encounters. He is generally a member of the gentry or upper class and embodies the aristocratic ideal of the gentleman, though this ideal is not necessarily the author's satiric norm. His associates are also invariably upper-class characters, if not aristocrats, who might be described as more "realistic" than characters of the third category. This third category comprises the grotesques, or eccentrics, who are usually but not invariably lower class and who are closer to caricature (the exaggeration of dominant traits) appropriate to farce.

II Body: Development of Argument

A. An examination of Waugh's fiction reveals that this threefold categorization can be more justly applied to his earlier fantasy-satires (*Decline and Fall*, *Vile Bodies*, etc.) than to his later works; however, it may still apply to the later works with the considerable adaptations determined by the different purposes of the narratives. For instance, Paul Pennyfeather in *Decline and Fall* is a good example of the naif, while Margot BesteChetwynde, her son Peter, and her lover Alastair Digby-Vaine-Trumpington comprise his associates; all of whom, it should be noted, figure in the **satire** although they are not grotesques. The grotesques make up the majority of the characters in *Decline and Fall*, and they figure largely in the "fantastic" quality of the **satire**. They range from the four major ones - Dr. Fagan, Grimes, Prendergast, and Philbrick- to minor figures like Margot's friend Chokey and Lady Circumference. All three categories, be it also noted, participate to varying degrees in a farcical plot.

B. In the second major work, *A Handful of Dust*, however, the action is not on the level of fantasy, and already a change in the categories becomes evident. The hero, Tony Last, is still a naif, but his naivete serves a subtler function. That is, his simple loyalty and decency still serves to "show up" the corruption of his wife Brenda and her lover John Beaver; but in addition, his blindness to reality, brought about by his complete absorption in his property, leads to his downfall. Branda, Beaver, and Jock all fit the category of associates. But the characters like the Vicar or Mr. Todd are not so much grotesques as more recognizable eccentrics in an action that is realistic rather than farcical.

C. In *Brideshead Revisited*, the first-person narrator is a naif adapted to the purpose of the narrative. Charles Ryder is not innocent of the world, but of the faith that he gradually discovers. Since the work is not a satire, however, his associates, in this case Sebastian and Julia and their family, are adapted to the author's different intention. They are aristocrats, but none is shown up as corrupt in contrast to Charles. And of the only figures who might correspond to grotesques (Charles' father and Anthony Patch), one is a semicaricature with no real part in the narrative and the other is a sexual deviate whose behavior accords with his personality.

D. And finally, *The Loved One*, returning to the mode of fantasy, employs a minimum of perfectly functional characters whose correspondence to the categories is far different from the early fantasies. Aimee is the naif whose pure devotion to the cult of Death destroys her, but except for this function she is far removed from the earlier **protagonists** or central figures. It could, in fact, be argued that Dennis is as much the **protagonist** in the sense that his is the central "consciousness" in the narrative, through whom most of the story is told. In addition, Dennis is an associate whose corruption is revealed by contrast to Aimee, but he is "upper-class" only in cultural attitude and education. And the last of the three main characters, Mr. Joyboy, is an associate as well as a grotesque whose grotesquerie is not individual but an embodiment of the society he represents.

III Conclusion: Summary of the Argument

It can justly be maintained, then, that the division of Waugh's characters into three basic categories, with the modifications required by the author's purpose, is evident in the four major works. Though each of the later works diverges from the earliest farcical **satire**, in each of them some version of the naif, along with the attendant associates and grotesques, can be discerned. And finally in the extent and variety of these adaptations can be discerned the dynamic quality of one of the most original and inventive imaginations in modern literature.

## EXERCISE QUESTIONS AND OUTLINES

1. How does the naif, or innocent central character, figure in Waugh's major works?

Outline:

I. The naif as "hero" or **protagonist** is found throughout, but with variations from the basic type as determined by the author's purpose.

II. Basic type exemplified by Paul Pennyfeather in *Decline and Fall* and by Tony Last in *A Handful of Dust*.

   a. Variant of the type in the "I" narrator of Brideshead Revisited, to suit the purpose of the **theme** of the conversion of the narrator.

   b. The Loved One illustrates a modification in Aimee, whose innocence is victimized by society.

III. The wide variety of the naif character indicates the adaptation of the basic satiric form to the author's purpose.

2. To what extent is A Handful of Dust different in kind from earlier **satires** like Decline and Fall?

Outline:

I. Although *A Handful of Dust* is often lumped with the earlier satires like *Decline and Fall*, the former are basically farce-fantasy and *A Handful of Dust* is ironic realism.

II. Illustration of farce-fantasy in exaggerated characters and improbable action of *Decline and Fall*.

   a. Illustration of ironic **realism** in realistic characters and ironic parallels and outcome of A Handful of Dust.

III. Despite the presence of farcical elements, which are integrated into the realistic context, A Handful of Dust is distinct from the earlier satire represented by Decline and Fall.

3. How does the prose style of Waugh's earlier **satires** differ from the later style of *Brideshead Revisited*?

Outline:

I. The difference between the prose style of his earliest **satire**, *Decline and Fall* and that of *Brideshead Revisited* is essentially one of a change not so much from simple to complex sentences as to a more extensive and complex imagery.

II. Illustrations of sentence structure in *Decline and Fall* and *Brideshead Revisited* reveal a lack of radical difference; also, the nostalgic descriptions in Brideshead are appropriate to the narrator.

    a. The use of dialogue in both is much the same.

    b. Differences in **imagery** illustrated by examples from *Decline and Fall* and *Brideshead Revisited*, especially the use of **metaphors** at the end of *Brideshead Revisited* to convey changes in character.

III. The so-called "later style" of *Brideshead Revisited*, which is rather peculiar to Brideshead than to all his later fiction, is different largely in its more extensive use of **imagery** to convey ideas.

4. What are the major differences between *Brideshead Revisited* and Waugh's earlier (pre-war) works?

Outline:

I. The major differences between *Brideshead Revisited* and the earlier works like *Decline and Fall* and *A Handful of Dust* can be reduced to three: (a) purpose; (b) point of view; and (c) characterization.

II. The purpose of the later work is not to satirize any group or institution, but rather to represent the process of religious conversion.

    a. The purpose leads to the choice of protagonist-as-narrator, the first-person point-of-view.

    b. The characterization is necessarily more complex than in the earlier novels because the **theme** depends on changes in behaviour and belief, and is not restricted to the function of satire.

III. The differences indicate that Waugh has actually created a form distinct from earlier (farcical or ironic) **satire**, a form that can be called "realistic romance."

5. If *The Loved One* is satiric fantasy, how does it differ from the earlier **satires** like *Decline and Fall*?

Outline:

I. That *The Loved One* is satiric fantasy is evident in the action (improbable and indeed "fantastic"), the characters (farcically exaggerated), and the purpose (to satirize the society represented by Whispering Glades).

II. However, it differs from the earlier **satires** like *Decline and Fall* in several important respects:

a. The main characters are not only fewer, numbering only three, but concentrate in themselves the functions that were earlier divided among a larger number of characters: Aimee is a naif, or innocent heroine, as well as a grotesque; Mr. Joyboy is an associate as well as a grotesque; and Dennis is the narrative **protagonist** as well as an associate.

b. With the exception of *A Handful of Dust*, the earlier **satires** had no identifiable norm, either implicit or explicit. The implied norm in *A Handful of Dust* is the ultimate spiritual value represented by the image of the City of God; but the implied norm in *The Loved One* is the whole body of Christian tradition indicated by its parody.

c. Stylistically, there is nothing in the work that does not contribute to the satiric purpose.

III. *The Loved One* differs from earlier works like *Decline and Fall* in its concentration of functions, pervasive norm, and stylistic economy - in sum, in the perfection of the form of satiric fantasy.

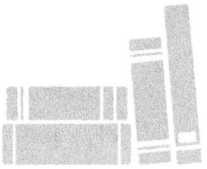

# A CRITICAL BIBLIOGRAPHY

## GUIDE TO FURTHER STUDY

Most of the criticism of Waugh's during his lifetime has been in the form of reviews, essays, and short studies. With growing recognition of his importance, full-length studies began to appear, though they are still relatively few in number. The following is a selective list of some of the more important criticism which will lead the interested student to other studies.

## Books

Carens, James F. *The Satiric Art of Evelyn Waugh*. The University of Washington Press, Seattle, 1966. The most complete general survey of Waugh's works that has appeared so far and the only one, as yet, that treats all of his last trilogy.

Bradbury, Malcolm. *Evelyn Waugh* (*Writers and Critics Series*). Oliver and Boyd, London, 1964. An interesting attempt to establish Waugh's satiric norm in an overall "comic tone," which the critic regards as consistent throughout Waugh's works.

Hollis, Christopher. *Evelyn Waugh* (*Writers and Their Work Series*: No. 46). Rev. ed., Longmans, Green & Co., London, 1958. A sympathetic survey by a lifelong friend and fellow-Catholic of Waugh's work up to the publication of the first volume of his final trilogy. It contains a fine, brief analysis of *The Loved One*.

Kermode, Frank. "Mr. Waugh's Cities" in *Puzzles and Epiphanies*. Routledge and Kegan Paul, London, 1962. Pp. 164-175. Kermode sees in Waugh's works generally, and in *Brideshead Revisited* specifically, an identification of the Catholic Faith with Western Culture. But the critic's identification of Hetton Abbey in *A Handful of Dust* with the City of God, or with eternal spiritual values, is questionable.

O'Donnell, Donat (Conor Cruise O'Brien). "The Pieties of Evelyn Waugh" in *Maria Cross: Imaginative Patterns in a Group of Modern Catholic Writers*. Oxford University Press, New York, 1952. Pp. 119-136. This important essay reveals the critic's bias against Waugh's aristocratic bias; it points to the origin of Waugh's **satire** in adolescent romanticism, but it fails to recognize the artistic development that often transcended the author's personal prejudices.

O'Faolain, Sean. *The Vanishing Hero*. Eyre and Spottiswoode, London, 1956. One of the best discussions of Waugh, it establishes the now common division between the "fantasy-satire" of his earlier period and the "realistic romance" of *Brideshead Revisited*. Noting the perennial power of the early satire, O'Faolain attributes it to an implicit and universally accepted norm; he ignores some of the inconsistencies in works like *Decline and Fall*.

Stopp, Frederic J. *Evelyn Waugh: Portrait of an Artist*. Little, Brown and Co., Boston, 1958. Another of the rare full-length studies done during Waugh's lifetime, it concludes with *The Ordeal of Gilbert Pinfold* (1957). Relating the author's works to his biography, it is a fascinating (if at times confusing) interpretation following the method of Jung's "mythological" analysis.

Waugh, Alec. *My Brother Evelyn and Other Portraits*. Farrar Straus and Giroux, New York, 1967. The title essay in the collection of memoirs, a touching tribute to abiding brotherly affection, is also important testimony to the strong religious strain in Evelyn, early noted by his elder brother, that became the central factor in his artistic development.

## Articles

Churchill, R. "Evelyn Waugh." *Encounter*, 31 (July 1968), 3-19. A brief biography.

Costello, Patrick. "An Idea of Comedy and Waugh's Sword of Honor." *Kansas Quarterly*, 1, No. 3 (1969), 41-50.

Davis, Robert M. "Textual Problems in the Novels of Evelyn Waugh." *Papers of the Bibliographic Society of America*, 63 (1969), 41-46.

Farr, D. Paul. "Evelyn Waugh: Tradition and a Modern Talent." *South Atlantic Quarterly*, 68 (1969), 506-19.

Wooton, Carl. "Evelyn Waugh's *Brideshead Revisited*: War and Limited Hope." *Midwest Quarterly*, 10 (1969), 359-75.

www.ingramcontent.com/pod-product-compliance
Lightning Source LLC
LaVergne TN
LVHW011729060526
838200LV00051B/3095